WORKING IN ADVERSARIAL RELATIONSHIPS

OPERATING EFFECTIVELY IN RELATIONSHIPS CHARACTERIZED BY LITTLE TRUST OR SUPPORT

Aryanne Oade
Director, Oade Associates Limited

palgrave
macmillan

First published 2011 by
PALGRAVE MACMILLAN

Palgrave Macmillan in the UK is an imprint of Macmillan Publishers Limited,
registered in England, company number 785998, of Houndmills, Basingstoke,
Hampshire RG21 6XS.

Palgrave Macmillan in the US is a division of St Martin's Press LLC,
175 Fifth Avenue, New York, NY 10010.

Palgrave Macmillan is the global academic imprint of the above companies
and has companies and representatives throughout the world.

Palgrave® and Macmillan® are registered trademarks in the United States,
the United Kingdom, Europe and other countries

ISBN 978-0-230-23843-5

This book is printed on paper suitable for recycling and made from fully
managed and sustained forest sources. Logging, pulping and manufacturing
processes are expected to conform to the environmental regulations of the
country of origin.

A catalogue record for this book is available from the British Library.

A catalog record for this book is available from the Library of Congress.

10 9 8 7 6 5 4 3 2 1
20 19 18 17 16 15 14 13 12 11

Printed and bound in Great Britain by
MPG Group, Bodmin and Kings Lynn

About the Author

Aryanne Oade has worked as a Chartered Psychologist since 1991. She has appeared on C4 speaking about customer complaints handling; has given an address on 'Creativity in Business' at the British Association for the Advancement of Science, and has appeared on Radio 4 speaking on the same topic. Aryanne has spoken at the Leeds and York Institute of Directors breakfast meetings on 'Politics, Power and Profit' and contributed to the Institute of Directors' *Director* magazine; and has given an address at the British Psychological Society's Annual Conference on 'Stress Levels Among South Yorkshire Probation Officers.' She is a member of the British Psychological Society's Special Group in Coaching Psychology and holds general membership at the Society's Division of Occupational Psychology. Aryanne is also a Member of the Association for Coaching.

Note from the Author

This book focuses on your skills and resolve while working in adversarial relationships. In writing the book I am not seeking to advise you, the reader, on how to handle your workplace relationships, but rather to offer you my experience and know-how as someone who has coached and worked with many clients on these issues. In addition to reading this book, you might want to seek the services and professional advice of a coach, business psychologist, or consultant, each of whom should be able to offer you tailored, detailed, and impartial counsel on the more challenging interpersonal and influencing issues you might face at work.

Acknowledgments

I would like to send my heartfelt thanks to a number of people.

Firstly, my deep gratitude goes to all the clients who have spoken with me over the years about their experiences of working in adversarial relationships. I am grateful to the very many of you who have shared with me your successes, frustrations, reactions, and strategies for managing adversarial colleagues and for handling these challenging colleagues and co-workers. Due my commitment to confidentiality I am not going to name any of you, but you know who you are, and I hope you will be able to own the thanks I would like to send to you anonymously.

Next, I would like to acknowledge the excellent value I received from the several clients and contacts that allowed me to pick their brains at the start of the writing process. These conversations were really great and helped me to decide how to structure and focus each of the chapters in the book. I send my thanks to each one of you gratefully and again, out of respect for confidentiality issues, anonymously.

Lastly, I would like to thank the banking executive who read the typescript for me at the end of the writing process and suggested an additional chapter which does, indeed, make the book more complete.

Overview

WHAT THIS BOOK IS ABOUT

This book is about working in adversarial relationships. It is about operating effectively in working relationships which are routinely characterized by little or no trust and support, and in which one party actively seeks to work against the other, no matter how closely structured their roles may be on the organization chart. The book is about how to work productively and wisely alongside and with co-workers whose job descriptions ought to involve them in working towards the same outcomes as you in broadly the same ways, but who are, in reality, actively pursuing their own internally derived, emotionally driven agenda which is in opposition to you and your concerns. This book is about how to manage this conflict on a day-to-day basis, and consequently how to operate effectively with adversarial colleagues, whether they are your managers, peers, or team members, and whether they use adversarial behavior on a selective or permanent basis.

The book focuses on the skills of working effectively with adversarial colleagues despite the challenges and the obstacles that their oppositional nature will inevitably create for you. It is about your willingness to use the specific behavior which will enable you to work within an adversarial relationship sufficiently well that you will be able to get done the things you need to get done by when you need to get them done, even though you are dealing with a colleague who:

- Is difficult and obstructive in nature.
- Will seek to undermine you when they perceive a suitable opportunity to do so.
- Is likely to actively work against you, at least some of the time.

The aim of the book is to equip you with the insight, skills, and strategies you need so that you can avoid the pitfalls that non-adversarial colleagues tend to make when working with an adversarial mindset, and so that more often than not you will:

- Become skilled at sizing up the dynamics of adversarial situations before deciding how to handle the characters and issues involved.

▪ Act in ways that will gain you the degree of influence you would like to have with an adversarial colleague.

▪ Retain a greater amount of energy and resolve for the aspects of your role that you most enjoy instead of seeing your enthusiasm dissipate as you struggle to manage an adversarial co-worker.

WHAT YOU WILL FIND IN THIS BOOK

I wrote this book for those of you who work with adversarial colleagues and who want to understand what practical actions you could take to better handle your adversarial co-worker. I believe that to be effective in an adversarial working relationship you need to develop a suite of people-handling skills and tactics relevant to that specific context. In particular you need to:

▪ Understand that using open, transparent behavior with an adversarial colleague could leave you vulnerable and lose you power, rather than gain you influence and respect, as would normally be the case.

▪ Recognize the irregular nature of the boundaries in adversarial relationships, respect them, and work actively within the room for maneuver that does exist.

▪ Develop a suite of people-handling skills specifically tailored to adversarial relationships that will enable you to get things done despite the challenges presented by these particular co-workers and workplace contacts.

I wrote this book for those of you who work in adversarial relationships at any level in an organization in any industry in any part of the world. The characteristics of adversarial relationships with which the book deals can be found in employees in any size of workplace, on any continent. These characteristics are not created by the particular industry in which you work or the number of colleagues you work alongside, although some industries may attract a greater proportion of people inclined to use adversarial approaches than others. Instead, the decision to adopt an adversarial attitude is down to the individual choice of the colleague who decides to do things this way.

So whether you work for a small, medium, or large organization, and no matter which industry or continent you work in, this book should help you to gain the insight, tactics, and skills you need to enable you to work more effectively and efficiently alongside adversarial colleagues.

MY BACKGROUND AND WORKPLACE EXPERIENCES

I am a Chartered Psychologist. I began working as a business psychologist in the late 1980s. During the following five years I worked for three consultancy firms before deciding to work as an independent business psychologist in early 1994. I made this move because I wanted to spend the greater part of my time working directly with clients, rather than managing colleague relationships. Some of my initial projects were carried out as an associate to smaller consultancy firms. Then, in January 2000, I set up Oade Associates to design and deliver bespoke executive coaching programs, tailored professional skills workshops, and custom-made conference scenarios.

In this work I combine business psychology with the skills of professional actors. We create real-life scenarios that reflect the leadership and influencing, negotiating and conflict resolution, political management and people-handling issues that my clients deal with in their day-to-day work. Since starting Oade Associates, I have run hundreds of executive coaching programs and professional skills workshops for managers and leaders working in the United Kingdom, Europe, and North America. Many of these projects have involved working with clients on the reality of selecting and using behavior that will prove effective in adversarial working relationships.

In my coaching programs and workshops I ask clients to step back from their day-to-day work and workplace experiences. I ask them to reflect on the quality of the behavior they use when things are going well for them, and to compare that with what they do when they are under pressure. Then, with the help of my professional actor colleagues, I recreate the very meetings clients find most challenging, meetings in which they need to handle the dynamics created by an adversarial colleagues, or in which they misinterpret the intent of adversarial colleagues, and unwittingly lose influence or credibility. I help clients to revisit these meetings using different and more productive behavior, skills, and tactics, behavior that is selected with the specific aim of enabling them to handle an adversarial situation.

I coach clients to understand the links between their intrapersonal world – their values, character, and personality – and their interpersonal behavior: the behaviors, tactics, skills, and strategies they use when working with an adversarial colleague. Clients practice their new approaches until they are satisfied that they can go back to work and use them straight away. As a result of working in this way clients perform better in their roles, have greater influence in their key workplace relationships, and demonstrate sustained behavior change.

In addition to working one-to-one and with small groups I also work with conference audiences. In this case I develop a series of custom-made sketches that my actor colleagues subsequently enact live on stage. Audience members discuss and debate the action at round tables, so that they can learn from one another's experiences of handling similar instances, and decide which interpersonal skills and tactics work well in particular situations and which don't.

This book comes out of my experience of helping many clients to develop the intrapersonal resolve and interpersonal dexterity they need to perform effectively when working with adversarial colleagues, and out of my belief that it is the quality of a person's people-handling skills, as opposed to their technical prowess, that largely determines who will gain and retain true influence with these tricky colleagues in the workplace.

How To Use This Book

WHAT THIS BOOK WILL DO FOR YOU

This book will guide you through a process whereby you make sense of and better understand behavior in your colleagues which is motivated by an adversarial mindset. It will enable you to identify a range of key behaviors and tactics regularly used by adversarial workplace contacts, and work through a process designed to help you decide how to handle these colleagues more effectively by:

- Learning how to read your colleagues' behavior more accurately.
- Recognizing what latitude does exist in an adversarial relationship, and determining how to work within that room for maneuver.
- Identifying where your adversarial colleagues prefer to put the boundary, and respecting that preference.
- Deciding who to negotiate with, over what, and how.
- Determining how to work with the uncollaborative, uncooperative, unsupportive agendas of the adversarial people with whom you need to form alliances to get things done.
- Recognizing the benefit of making it your business to find solutions to selected issues that are impeding your progress against your goals, even if it will involve some considerable effort on your part to engage with the adversarial characters who have created those circumstances.

This book will take you through a process of stepping back from your day-to-day work and considering how you go about influencing and working with key adversarial colleagues. It will help you to re-evaluate how you initiate contact with and respond to contact from adversarial colleagues, and encourage you to reassess how you seek to build influence and work alongside them. You will learn what you need to do to differently and handle better a range of colleagues who have a competitive and uncooperative mindset. As a result of reading this book you should be better placed to:

■ Build alliances – however fragile – to get specific things done at work.

■ Recognize impending pressure points in workplace adversarial relationships and act accordingly.

■ Use your energy wisely to influence key adversarial colleagues.

■ Position yourself as an influential member of the workforce – at least on selected key issues.

■ Resolve the workplace conflicts that you need to tackle and which you might otherwise lack the confidence or know-how to resolve.

■ Use an increased range of options for generating momentum when your adversarial colleagues act in ways that prevent progress, impede action, and create inertia in your work.

THE CASE STUDIES

From Chapter 1 onwards, the book introduces you to a series of case studies, each of which mirrors realistic dynamics found in adversarial working relationships. These case studies illustrate the pitfalls, mistakes, oversights, and errors of judgment that can lose you influence and harm your credibility when working with an adversarial colleague. They also provide you with a blueprint for how to go about maximizing the influence you could have in a range of adversarial situations. A few of these scenarios are based on real-life dynamics or are an amalgam of several real-life situations. Because of my commitment to working in a way that honors client confidentiality, in each of these instances the details of the characters, the setting of the events, and the specific details of the scenarios have been completely fictionalized to protect the identities of the people involved.

Following an outline of the key facts in a case study you will find a section entitled 'Analyzing the Dynamics.' This section will take you behind the action to describe the motives and conclusions of the main character as they engage with the dynamics in the scenario. This section will identify issues facing the main character as they deal with their adversarial colleague, as well as highlighting the risks that this character faces should they mishandle the situation. It will also take a deeper look at the personality of the adversarial colleague whom the main character needs to work alongside. We will also identify those factors that would or would not prove persuasive with a particular adversarial character's personality. This section will get behind their actions, words, and behaviors to understand their motivations and intentions, and identify the best ways to handle them and work alongside them.

YOUR ADVERSARIAL COLLEAGUES

Periodically, the book will invite you to consider your responses to a series of questions about your adversarial co-workers – and, sometimes, your own use of adversarial behavior. Each question is followed by a space in the text so that you can jot down your answer to it if you want to. These questions will provide you with an opportunity to apply the key points from the previous sections of the book to your working life, helping you get the most out of the process of reading the material. These sections will encourage you to step back from your day-to-day work and:

- Review how you currently engage and work with a range of adversarial managers, peers, and team members.
- Identify what opportunities and risks exist in those relationships.
- Make decisions about what to do to improve the way in which you handle your relationships with these key workplace contacts.

NARRATIVE CASE STUDY

The final chapter of the book takes the form of a narrative case study. The case study follows the progress of a newly promoted training manager working for a fictional clothing manufacturer. The action centers on how he gets to grips with the highly political environment he encounters among the top team to whom he now reports, an environment created by the series of adversarial alliances which these senior players generate with one another. The case study illustrates the tensions that exist between the newly promoted employee and one key internal client, an adversarial character whose tactics take the training manager by surprise and threaten to damage his reputation with his senior team. As you read the narrative you will be asked to analyze it from the point of view of the training manager to determine what you think he could do differently to better handle the situation he finds himself in.

Following each portion of the case study you will find a section entitled 'Questions for You to Answer' and a space below each question so that you can jot down your responses to it. You will also find suggested answers to these questions at the end of the case study, against which you can compare and contrast your own ideas. These answers will provide you with tips, tactics, skills, and strategies which could be used to interpret and respond to the instances of adversarial behavior described in the narrative.

Contents

**1 What is an Adversarial Working Relationship? The
Behaviors and Dynamics in a Relationship Characterized
by Little Trust or Support**   **1**
Your experience of adversarial working relationships   1
An adversarial colleague: a definition   3
Exploring adversarial workplace relationships   3
The mindset of an adversarial colleague   4
An adversarial colleague: a contradiction in terms?   6
The consequences of adversarial behavior for the workplace   6
Case study 1: First encounter   8
    First encounter: analyzing the dynamics   8
Case study 2: Covering up   11
    Covering up: analyzing the dynamics   12
Summary and next chapter   16

**2 The Impact of Adversarial Behavior at Work: The
Consequences of Oppositional Behavior for Workplace
Relationships**   **17**
Adversarial politicians, adversarial bullies   17
The dynamics created by an adversarial colleague   20
The quality of relationships created by adversarial
    behavior   21
Case study 3: Answering the question   22
    Answering the question: analyzing the dynamics   23
The challenge of working with an adversarial colleague   26
The consequences of adversarial working environments   27
Case study 4: Altered agenda   28
    Altered agenda: analyzing the dynamics   29
Your adversarial colleagues   32
Summary and next chapter   34

**3 Low Trust, Low Support: The Cornerstones of an
Adversarial Approach**   **35**
The role of trust and support at work   35
The links between support and challenge   37
Support and challenge in your work   38

The challenge presented by adversarial colleagues   40
Different people, different expressions of support   42
Case study 5: Working without trust   43
    Working without trust: analyzing the dynamics   44
Your adversarial colleagues   47
Summary and next chapter   48

4   Selective Adversarial Behavior: Colleagues who Sometimes Use an Adversarial Approach and who Sometimes Don't   49
The decision to use selective adversarial behavior   49
The impact of selective adversarial behavior   51
Case study 6: Change of heart   51
    Change of heart: analyzing the dynamics   53
Case study 7: Overstepping the mark   56
    Overstepping the mark: analyzing the dynamics   58
Boundary conflicts: a key underlying issue   61
Case study 8: Addressing the issues   61
    Addressing the issues: analyzing the dynamics   62
Addressing the issues: a word of warning   63
Your adversarial colleagues   64
Summary and next chapter   65

5   Working with Adversarial Peers: Minimizing the Risk of Working without Authority and with Little Influence   67
Handling an adversarial peer   68
Case study 9: Fishy business   69
    Fishy business: analyzing the dynamics   71
Managing the boundaries   76
Finding suitable boundaries: three short examples   77
Managing the boundaries around your work   81
Retaining control of work you are managing   82
Your adversarial colleagues   83
Case study 10: Cutting through the fog   84
    Cutting through the fog: analyzing the dynamics   86
Circumventing an oppositional streak   89
Case study 11: Ganging up   91
    Ganging up: analyzing the dynamics   93
Your adversarial colleagues   97
Summary and next chapter   98

6 Managing an Adversarial Team Member: Confronting Counterproductive Behavior   **99**

Handling an adversarial team member   99
Case study 12: Provoking disagreement   100
   Provoking disagreement: analyzing the dynamics   101
The signals of an adversarial team member   103
Dodging the issue   104
Case study 13: Confrontation   105
   Confrontation: analyzing the dynamics   106
Naming the game   109
Your adversarial colleagues   110
Case study 14: Rebel mode   112
   Rebel mode: analyzing the dynamics   113
Antagonism towards authority   116
Case study 15: Generous spirit   118
   Generous spirit: analyzing the dynamics   118
Giving feedback to an adversarial team member   121
Your adversarial colleagues   123
Summary and next chapter   124

7 Reporting to an Adversarial Manager: Handling a Boss with Organizational Authority and an Adversarial Mindset   **125**

Comparing an adversarial manager and a non-adversarial
   manager   127
   How a non-adversarial manager uses their organizational
      authority   127
   How an adversarial manager uses their organizational
      authority   129
   The impact of adversarial managers   131
   Lower levels of trust and support   132
Case study 16: Managing the manager   133
   Managing the manager: analyzing the dynamics   134
Your adversarial colleagues   136
The aim of an adversarial manager   137
The challenge of working for an adversarial manager   138
Case study 17: Straight answer to a straight question   139
   Straight answer to a straight question: analyzing the
      dynamics   140
The mindset of an adversarial manager   143
Case study 18: Creating a senior enemy   145
   Creating a senior enemy: analyzing the dynamics   147

Making your points and losing less   151
Mitigating the risks of compliance   152
Your adversarial colleagues   154
Case19: Keeping your eye on the ball   155
    Keeping your eye on the ball: analyzing the dynamics   156
Keep on doing what you usually do   157
Summary and next chapter   159

8 Adversarial Allies: A Narrative Case Study   161
Moving up   161
Meeting the senior team   162
Attending the top team meeting   164
Questions for you to answer: set one   165
Working with the brand team   166
Last-minute hitch   167
Questions for you to answer: set two   168
The team assessment workshop   168
Questions for you to answer: set three   170
Six questions   170
Questions for you to answer: set four   172
Picking up the pieces   173
Questions for you to answer: set five   174
The sales director's response   174
Fallout   175
Questions for you to answer: set six   176
Review section: answers to the questions   177
    Set one   177
    Set two   179
    Set three   182
    Set four   183
    Set five   185
    Set six   187

References and Recommended Reading   *193*
Index   *195*

What is an Adversarial Working Relationship?

The Behaviors and Dynamics in a Relationship Characterized by Little Trust or Support

Let's begin this book by considering what an 'adversarial working relationship' means. We will define the term and explore some of the characteristics of an adversarial workplace relationship. We will examine the specific dynamics that might be involved in a working relationship that is adversarial, and describe what issues these dynamics might create for those of you who get caught up in a relationship best characterized by low levels of trust, low levels of support, and some degree of opposition. We will also examine your own experiences of working within these kinds of relationships and illustrate the characteristics of adversarial working relationships using a number of realistic examples.

So let's start with you and your experiences of adversarial workplace relationships. Specifically, at the commencement of this first chapter, let's focus for a few minutes on:

- Your attitude to workplace relationships and to activity that you consider to be adversarial
- The consequences you observe in your workplace of adversarial behavior.

YOUR EXPERIENCE OF ADVERSARIAL WORKING RELATIONSHIPS

What does the phrase 'adversarial working relationship' conjure up for you? You might like to take a few minutes to jot down in the space below any phrases and words that come to mind when you consider the term:

You might now like to consider the workplace consequences of the adversarial conduct you observe around you. You can use the space below to write down your thoughts:

Whatever words you wrote in the two spaces above, and however difficult or straightforward you found it to capture what an adversarial working relationship means to you, the key thing to note is that it only takes one person to create an adversarial element in a workplace. It only takes one colleague to act in an adversarial way towards one of their colleagues once for the character of that relationship to change, and for colleagues observing the adversarial activity to become aware that their own relationship with that co-worker might be similarly affected in the future. Depending on the seniority of the person using the adversarial tactics, their activity might also have an impact on the very culture of the workplace.

From the moment that adversarial intent is introduced into a workplace, colleagues affected by it or observing it are likely to think that from that moment onwards they:

■ Will have to be watchful and aware of the motives of their adversarial co-worker.
■ Would do well to be more cautious and careful around that person.
■ Can't really trust that colleague in the way you would have done before they used adversarial behavior.
■ Are unlikely to behave in an unguarded and open way towards them in the future.
■ Now regard their relationship with that person as having moved into different territory, territory characterized by their colleague's potential enmity towards them as a person rather than by their pursuit of organizational goals relevant to their job descriptions.

AN ADVERSARIAL COLLEAGUE: A DEFINITION

What is an adversarial colleague? Consider the following three-part definition:

- An adversarial colleague is one who uses behavior that erodes trust at work while introducing a level of personalized enmity into a working relationship with a manager, peer, or team member.
- This colleague does not act in line with their workplace requirement to build and maintain effective relationships with co-workers for the good of their employer, but handles their workplace relationships as a series of separate and discrete transactions.
- This colleague's behavior precludes much, or sometimes any, trust being developed or maintained with their co-workers and necessarily results in low levels of support existing in their relationships. Trust and support are likely to remain at low levels throughout the period during which a relationship is characterized by this colleague's transactional approach towards other people at work.

EXPLORING ADVERSARIAL WORKPLACE RELATIONSHIPS

So an adversarial working relationship is one in which, in structural terms, two colleagues are apparently working together to achieve aims and objectives of value to their employer. The problem is that at least one them behaves in an inimical way towards the other, either frequently or infrequently. The emotion that at least one of the colleagues introduces into the relationship results in that person using behavior which prevents usual levels of trust forming or being maintained, and precludes supportive exchanges between the two co-workers. This colleague sometimes or always personalizes their animosity towards their co-worker in a series of inimical or antagonistic acts which, depending on the severity and frequency of the actions taken, further damage the relationship and turn it into one marked by ongoing enmity and opposition.

Should the relationship become one that is consistently adversarial it is no longer about two people working towards joint aims for the good of their employer. It is now about one or both colleagues' antipathy towards their co-worker, their co-worker's methods, or their co-worker's aims, a state of affairs which results in either or both of them placing higher priority on acting on these instincts rather than any other set of workplace considerations. Under these circumstances business decisions about:

- Improving customer service
- Enhancing internal processes
- Creating new and better products or services

are subordinated under the adversarial colleague's wish to act against their colleague, even if that colleague remains committed to acting in the best interests of their employer and therefore uses non-adversarial behavior.

Incidents of a colleague using adversarial behavior could occur infrequently and with only one selected colleague; or could be a fixed, firm feature of a colleague's workplace behavior with everyone; or could occur anywhere on the continuum in between.

THE MINDSET OF AN ADVERSARIAL COLLEAGUE

Why would anyone choose to handle their workplace relationships like this? Every adversarial colleague is unique and will have their own individual reasons for acting as they do. But it is probably the case that for most colleagues using adversarial behavior represents a misguided attempt to feel safe. It is likely that most adversarial colleagues approach their workplace relationships in this way because they are trying to avoid placing themselves in a position in which they will be vulnerable to:

- Feeling exposed or unsafe.
- Being let down.
- Being used by a colleague.
- Losing control.

They do this by arranging their workplace relationships so that they don't establish or maintain trust with anyone, don't offer support to anyone or easily receive offers of support from anyone either, and in the hope that if they keep their connections loose, ill-defined, and devoid of trust they will be less vulnerable. Their conduct can therefore come across to their colleagues as lacking usual levels of commitment to and responsibility towards their co-workers or their co-workers' work. In and of itself this is difficult enough. But add to it a desire to act against selected colleagues on an occasional or frequent basis for any number of reasons, and you have an adversarial colleague who can be a nightmare to work for or alongside.

Adversarial colleagues may or may not come to regard offers of trust and support at work as weak or risible, but whatever their attitude to them, they eschew them out of fear that to form a connection with a colleague, however tentative, would place them at risk. Being unwilling to extend trust to colleagues, they then don't react well to offers of trust, which they usually reject. Equally, not feeling comfortable accepting support they don't offer much either. In this sense adversarial colleagues are actually trying to prevent themselves being taken advantage of, but only succeed in setting up a workplace dynamic in which they promote enmity and opposition by pushing their colleagues away and failing to engage with them productively. This makes it more, not less, likely that they will annoy a co-worker or let someone else down sufficiently badly that they increase the likelihood of the kind of political maneuver they fear being used against them.

In addition, adversarial colleagues often introduce a degree of oppositional behavior into their workplace relationships. From time to time they deliberately act against their co-workers simply because they can, simply because they want to and because it serves their purpose to give notice to their colleagues that they are real foes not to be messed with.

Not all adversarial colleagues will operate at the end of the continuum described above. Some will have less marked adversarial traits. Others may only employ these tactics over certain issues or with certain colleagues whom they view with particular suspicion. However, it is a sad fact that adversarial colleagues can unconsciously create the very set of circumstances that they want to avoid, and having set themselves up in this way, usually don't recognize the vital role that they have played in setting up these dynamics in the first place. Not recognizing their pivotal role, they continue to blame others, regarding their colleagues as untrustworthy and unreliable. Blind to their own untrustwhiness, they continue with their transactional tactics and fail to take advantage of opportunities to handle things in a more open, transparent and relationally engaged way. This creates further tension in their relationships and so the cycle continues. Adversarial colleagues truly are their own worst enemies. They create opposition and hostility in their workplace relationships where, if they used a different approach, there wouldn't be as much.

AN ADVERSARIAL COLLEAGUE: A CONTRADICTION IN TERMS?

Those of you who regard 'an adversarial colleague' as a contradiction in terms may well have a point. To a non-adversarial mindset it is a contradiction in terms to turn your enmity on the very people you should be working with to achieve success for your employer. Those of you who think this way might regard the word 'colleague' has having connotations of 'collegiality' or 'partnership' or 'collaboration,' and might find the use of adversarial behavior destructive and baffling. However, to an adversarial co-worker the two concepts of 'enemy' and 'colleague' sit together quite comfortably without causing any internal conflict.

An adversarial colleague is comfortable working against their workplace associates in a variety of smaller and larger ways, and doesn't see any contradiction in this way of doing things. In fact, some adversarial colleagues only know how to do things this way. They may literally have no prior experiences of being in trusting or supportive relationships either inside or outside work. Without a doubt, their approach makes it very difficult for them to develop workplace relationships characterized by either trusting or supportive behavior. But the key point is that lacking experiences of these kinds of healthy and fruitful workplace connections, they don't know how to develop them and may well have come to regard them as unimportant or contemptible. They may even look down upon co-workers who are adept at developing rapport or mutual liking and respect. They may regard these qualities with suspicion and be motivated to cut the colleagues who display them down to size. Adversarial mindsets are truly the mindsets of people stuck wielding a double-edged sword. They create and promote enmity, and each time they succeed in handling things this way, take themselves further away from the kinds of productive and effective workplace connections that they are being paid to establish and which it would be beneficial to them to experience and maintain.

THE CONSEQUENCES OF ADVERSARIAL BEHAVIOR FOR THE WORKPLACE

Having defined what we mean by an adversarial colleague, and begun to describe the adversarial mindset, let's now explore some of the consequences for the workplace of adversarial behavior. Then we will apply the definition given above to two separate examples so we can see the difference between a manager acting in an adversarial way and a manager being very difficult to deal with but not actually being adversarial.

Those of you who recognize the above description, either from behavior which adversarial colleagues have employed towards you or from observing such methods being employed around your workplace, may be concerned about the impact that this way of doing things has on the character of your organization. Remembering that the motivation behind adversarial behavior is to personalize opposition to specific colleagues while maintaining low levels of support and trust, how many of the following consequences of adversarial behavior do you recognize from your workplace? An adversarial colleague is likely to become adept at:

- Blocking progress on key issues and obstructing open debate on important topics, especially if doing these things will create inconvenience for specific colleagues.
- Raising unnecessary and time-consuming objections that delay decisions or render them more difficult to make.
- Impeding decision-making and problem-solving processes by creating fog around the key concerns or otherwise finding ways to hinder progress.
- Putting forward contrary viewpoints simply to object to or attack other people's input.
- Niggling away at specific co-workers' ideas, reputations, and resolve.
- Creating dissent, disagreements, and disputes instead of concentrating on resolving issues and creating momentum.
- Failing to address points put to them in meetings, preferring to answer different and often unrelated points instead.
- Taking advantage of opportunities to badmouth colleagues or shift blame onto them inappropriately.

You may well to able to add to this list, which is not intended to be exhaustive. But the key point is that none of these outcomes is positive. Rarely does anyone comment that one of the consequences of having an adversarial co-worker is that it improves the workplace and creates positive results for its employees and customers. Rather it is the implications of working with little or no trust and support, and the consequences of overt or simmering antagonism, that concern the colleagues of adversarial co-workers. It is the:

- Wasted effort
- Escalated conflicts
- Missed deadlines
- Demoralizing effect of bothersome or more forthright arguments

that wear down the resolve and enthusiasm of those caught up in the dynamics of adversarial workplace relationships. Consider the following example.

CASE STUDY 1: FIRST ENCOUNTER

During a selection interview process a potential new recruit to a niche insurance firm meets the manager to whom he would report should he take up the role. The interview goes well and he is offered the position. During the contract negotiations with his new boss later that day he agrees five key improvements to the initial contract he is offered, and consents to join the firm in four weeks' time. Three weeks into this period his manager sends him the amended contract via email. The new recruit is surprised to notice that the contract does not reflect any of the five changes he had verbally agreed with his new boss. In fact, it is a replica of the original contract and is unaltered from it. He telephones his new boss to point out what has happened. His boss is short with him, but not rude. He says that he will send through an amended contract. Sure enough, ten minutes later, a new email arrives with a contract attached. The new recruit reads it and is astonished to note that the new contract only contains one of the five improvements and amendments he was expecting, but not any of the other four.

First Encounter: Analyzing the Dynamics

Let's revisit this situation and analyze the dynamics in it so we can form a view as to whether this boss is or is not behaving in an adversarial way.

In this example the boss verbally agrees to a series of contractual amendments with his new recruit but doesn't produce the new contract for three weeks. When he does send the contract through he sends a replica of the original document, a version that does not contain any of the five amendments and improvements to which he had previously verbally agreed. At this stage the new recruit decides to act with caution and leave room for the possibility that his new boss has made an innocent error. He could be over-worked, poor with detail or otherwise not on top of things.

Aware that his actions could simply be the result of an oversight, the recruit calls his soon-to-be boss to point out the omissions from the contract. He hears his boss say that he will send through a new version of the document. Sure enough, he does do so, but the version of the contract he sends through only contains one of the five amendments and not all five as the new recruit expects. He has sent through an amended contract but not the one the new recruit agreed to.

Rather than give him the benefit of the doubt a second time, the new recruit realizes that he is about to commence working for a manager who is distinctly untrustworthy. He forms the view that the boss's actions are likely quite purposeful. He doesn't think that the manager has a problem with any of the five amendments in themselves. It is much more likely that he simply wants to know how far he can push his new recruit from the off.

The new recruit realizes these things and decides that there is an oppositional and ambivalent side to this manager, one that causes him to demonstrate a basic lack of integrity and lack of basic honesty when he is minded to do so.

But in what ways do his actions constitute adversarial conduct? Let's revisit the three-part definition and apply it to the action:

- First, does the manager behave in ways which erode trust and support and which introduce a level of personalized enmity into the relationship? Yes, he does. The manager makes a series of verbal agreements with his new recruit, agreements which he subsequently fails to act in line with. When his error is pointed out to him he doesn't come clean and take responsibility for his mistake. He doesn't take advantage of the opportunity to apologize for his error and get the working relationship off on a positive footing. He can't do these things because he hasn't made an error. He has acted deliberately and with forethought, and he isn't at all sorry. This is clear evidence of his untrustworthy and unsupportive nature, and clear evidence of a level of groundless enmity on his part towards his new recruit.
- Second, does the manager disregard his workplace responsibility to build and maintain an effective relationship with his new recruit and instead handle his relationship with him as a series of disconnected transactions? Yes, he does. In his first meeting with the new recruit at the selection interview the manager agrees certain changes to the contract. But when it comes down to it he

disregards this conversation entirely and sends through a version of the contract that is unaltered from the original. He acts as if the previous conversation hadn't happened. The contract does not reflect the five agreed changes and is not the one to which the new recruit agreed to work. But the boss sends it anyway. Furthermore, when his new recruit points out this situation to him in a telephone call the boss is clipped in his response, not apologetic. He takes no responsibility for what he has done and merely says he will send through an amended contract. This is tricky wording on his part because while he does send through an amended contract it only reflects one of the five agreed amendments. Once more, he has disconnected the content of the conversation he has just had from his subsequent actions. Even though he did explicitly say, 'I will send through a version of the contract that contains all five amendments' it is quite obvious that this is what is called for. But, even though this conversation took place only a matter of minutes earlier and he cannot have forgotten it, the boss only makes one of the five amendments before sending the contract through. Either he hopes that his new recruit won't notice the omission of the other four amendments, or he hopes that his recruit will lack the resolve to call him a second time and have the same conversation again. These actions are evidence of a manager who is untrustworthy in nature and adversarial in intent. Even though he has clearly agreed to five contract amendments he ignores these imperatives and does what he wants to do for reasons only he will truly understand. He does not do what he says he will do, and when called on his deceit, compounds his original untrustworthy acts with further instances of duplicity. These actions illustrate the degree to which this manager wants to act in line with his transactional, adversarial nature rather than in line with more usual workplace criteria such as establishing liking and respect with a new recruit or handling contractual arrangements with transparency and honesty.

■ Third, does the manager's conduct make it likely that low levels of trust and support will become a feature of the relationship? Yes, they do. The manager's decision to test the boundaries of his new recruit's resolve before he joins the workforce is a clear indication of what working for him will be like should the new recruit decide to go ahead and take the job. His would-be manager can have no reason to hold a grudge against a person with whom he has he had very little contact and to whom he has offered a job in his team. He can have no real justification for feeling enmity towards him. His decision to trap his new colleague into a contract he does not want and did not agree to can only be motivated by his own antagonistic nature, and is a clear warning of his propensity to use behavior that precludes the formation of trust and support. It is highly likely that working with this manager would involve having to operate without either trust or support for long periods of time. Only the new recruit can decide whether or not he is up for this challenge, but if he has had no previous experience of working for a boss who handles things in this way, he will not know what the day-to-day reality of it will be like until he has accepted the post.

We can say quite clearly that this manager is, in this instance, behaving in an adversarial way. We can conclude that his conduct towards the new recruit is motivated by his own inimical, transactional nature rather than by what we would expect: a wish to establish a mutually productive working relationship with a new colleague. While his conduct does not automatically imply that he will *always and only* handle his workplace affairs as a series of disconnected transactions, it does represent a big warning that he might be capable of doing things in this way. The new recruit can still go ahead and work for this boss if he wants to, having insisted that his contract be amended fully to reflect their previous agreement. But he will need to do so with his eyes wide open as to the disposition of his new manager. In a way his manager's actions have been helpful to the new recruit. He has actually behaved in an adversarial way towards his new employee *before* he even joins the organization, and has fully alerted his potential new colleague to the reality of his adversarial, transactional instincts.

Having explored an example of a manager acting in an adversarial way towards a new recruit, let's now examine a second example. Consider the following scenario which describes a case of behavior that is not adversarial but which is still highly taxing to deal with.

CASE STUDY 2: COVERING UP

Two departmental heads are engaged in agreeing a service level agreement (SLA) to enable them to cooperate in achieving more stretching delivery targets. Following a history of incomplete and inaccurate data being sent by the staff of the first departmental head to the team run by the second departmental head, the second head suggests that the SLA ought to include a clause specifying what will happen in future should further error-ridden data find its way to his team. The first departmental head shows a moue of distaste for the suggestion that his department might 'make mistakes.' He says he will get back to his colleague, stands up and abruptly leaves the room before his peer can say anything further. When he does get back to his colleague later on that day it is via email. He makes the point that 'my interpretation of mistakes is different from yours' before declining to include any wording in the SLA that would clarify a procedure for handling errors or omissions.

On reading the email his colleague feels discomfited and unsettled. He dislikes the snide wording of the email, feels that he has been wrongfooted somehow and doesn't know what to do next to achieve the outcome he wants. He forms the view that his colleague doesn't want to acknowledge the extent of the sloppy work produced by his staff and is not minded to take ownership of the consequences of his department's dilatory approach for his own team members. Furthermore, he realizes that this colleague has moved the conversation between them away from a collaborative conversation about improving delivery targets into different territory, territory characterized by his wish to cover up his department's poor standards by omitting a key section from the SLA.

Covering Up: Analyzing the Dynamics

Let's revisit this situation and analyze the dynamics in it so we can form a view as to whether this boss is or is not an adversarial colleague.

In this example two departmental heads agree to produce a SLA detailing how their two teams will work together to enhance delivery standards. However, they hit a snag when one of the two heads suggests that the SLA needs to include a section outlining a procedure to handle mistakes made by either department, mistakes which will inevitably affect the quality of work done by the other department. His colleague makes clear his distaste for this suggestion and unexpectedly leaves the room. When he re-engages with his colleague later in the day he does so on email, using a confusing form of words to suggest that his interpretation of mistakes differs from his colleague's and to decline to include any wording in the SLA that would cover errors and their consequences.

At this point the department head reading the email is nonplussed. He feels that the ground has shifted under his feet. The phraseology used by his colleague – 'my interpretation of mistakes is different from yours' – appears to question *his* judgment and to insinuate that *he* is trying to make more of the issue than he ought to. It implies that *he*, the peer reading the email, is in the wrong and that he mistrusts his colleague and his team unjustly. It is a confusing and inexact form of words which succeeds in creating unease in the mind of the head of department reading the email without saying anything specific. However, it is a form of words that clearly points the finger at him and is quite clearly evidence of a degree of personalized irritation with him on the part of his colleague. While the departmental head realizes that his colleague is acting to cover up the inadequacies in his department he also feels thrown and doesn't know what to do next to move things forward. He is faced with two options: try to reopen the issue of the additional clause which, given the contents of the email and his colleague's prior conduct in leaving the meeting, seems a fruitless line to take, or accommodate his colleague's wishes and leave out of the SLA a clause which is important to him and which he would rather include in it.

His basic difficulty lies in the fact that he thought the two of them were working together to write a jointly agreed SLA. In the spirit of this joint activity he asks for something specific to be incorporated into the SLA, a section covering mistakes and errors, something important to him, his department and their employing organization given its current drive to improve service standards. He does so assuming that the request will be met with interest and openness. However, he now realizes that his, to his mind, perfectly reasonable request pressed a red button in the psyche of his colleague, who then reacted by blocking all debate on the issue.

Is this an example of adversarial behavior or merely an example of behavior that, while very difficult to handle, is not actually adversarial? Let's revisit the three-part definition and apply it to the action to find out:

- First, does the defensive departmental head behave in ways which erode trust and support and which introduce a level of personalized enmity into the relationship? Only partly. The two departmental heads initially work together well on the SLA and only run into trouble when the issue of mistakes is brought up by one of them. The defensive peer decides to walk out of the room and subsequently sends a confusing email to his colleague, an email which inevitably alters the level of trust between them and reduces the level of support between them. However, the defensive peer's motive for doing this is not purely the product of a level of enmity towards his colleague. Nor is it a desire on his part to preserve a level of transactional contact between them. He does so because he is concerned that, should the SLA include a section on handling errors, a number of senior managers in the wider organization might realize that there is a cause for concern in his department. His conduct is therefore not about introducing groundless antagonism into the relationship between himself and his peer, although it could be seen this way. Nor is it about an attempt to see how far he can push his peer, although it could be seen that way too. Instead, it is a clumsy attempt to protect himself from possible exposure as a sloppy and dilatory manager. His behavior is therefore not evidence of a basically untrustworthy and unsupportive nature in the defensive manager. Nor is it evidence that he carries a level of animosity towards his colleague. Instead, it is simply a crude attempt at self-protection, and one so poorly executed that it could leave him open to being seen as acting in an adversarial way whether or not he intends to do so.

■ Second, does the defensive manager disregard his workplace responsibility to maintain an effective relationship with his peer and instead handle his relationship with him as a series of disconnected transactions? Only partly. As a manager, and as a manager actively engaged in a piece of work designed to enhance delivery standards, the defensive departmental head does indeed have a duty to his employer to explore every way of raising the bar. Because he is doing so in tandem with his peer, he also needs to work well with him. From the moment he walks out of the room he fails to do either of these things well. He ignores the opportunity to address the number of mistakes in his department by including a section covering these issues in the SLA, and thereby fails his employer. But his motive for ignoring this responsibility is not because he wants to handle his peer in a transactional way. Rather his motivation is his fear that his dilatory approach to managing his department will be exposed, and as a basically lazy man, he doesn't want to go there. It is quite possible that on any subsequent piece of joint work with his peer he will be amendable to work with, although whether his peer will trust him in the same way again remains to be seen. So while there is evidence that the defensive head of department acts in an obstructive and awkward way over the issue of mistakes in the SLA, there is no evidence that he does this to reduce his relationship with his peer to a series of adversarial transactions.

■ Third, does the defensive manager's conduct make it likely that low levels of trust and support will become a feature of the relationship? Again, maybe and maybe not. The moment the defensive departmental head sends his email to his peer he alters the dynamic between them. He signals a change in their working arrangements on this piece of work, from one in which they can get things done together to one in which he pushes his colleague away from him, hoping that his actions will stall the SLA and he can avoid the need to reduce the number of errors coming from his department. These actions do alter the level of cooperation between them and they do create tension in the relationship. But do they mean that the entire relationship from that moment onwards will be characterized by low levels of trust and support? Probably not, but it does depend on the extent to which the non-defensive peer understands that his colleague's actions are motivated by fear and are not aimed at him personally; and on the extent to which the two of them are prepared to work together to re-establish a viable way of getting things done in the future. The defensive peer would have been much wiser to avoid creating so much confusion by addressing his irresponsibility as a manager, his lack of willingness to manage his department to a high standard, and his lazy attitude to mistakes, rather than create a hiatus in his relationship with his colleague. So while the defensive peer has succeeded in interrupting the dialogue between him and his colleague, he hasn't done so with the intention of impairing the levels of trust and support that exist between them. There is a risk that the levels of both trust and support between them will be eroded because of the way he handles the issues before him, but he does not act this way solely to bring about this outcome.

So while in the first example the manager could reasonably be seen as an adversarial colleague, it would be hard to lay that charge at the door of the departmental head in the second example, no matter how poorly he has handled the issues before him, and how challenging and vexing his behavior is to deal with.

These are fine discriminations to make but they are vital ones if you are to understand the intent of your colleague correctly and therefore select and use the most effective interpersonal tool for handling their behavior. The rest of the book will focus on equipping you with a range of interpersonal tactics for handling adversarial behavior so that you will know what to do when you next find yourself in a situation in which a colleague's conduct is motivated by an adversarial mindset.

SUMMARY AND NEXT CHAPTER

This chapter has concentrated on defining adversarial behavior and exploring the difference between adversarial and non-adversarial intent. It has highlighted some of the consequences for the workplace of adversarial conduct, and provided you with opportunities to consider what behaviors adversarial colleagues might use in your workplace, and what outcomes these behaviors may create for you and your colleagues. The chapter has suggested that making an accurate judgment about whether or not the motivation of a particular colleague is or is not adversarial is vital if you are to handle their behavior effectively.

The next chapter will examine in greater detail the mindset of adversarial colleagues. It will consider more fully the dynamics they create in their workplaces and explore the quality of the relationships they seek to build at work.

CHAPTER 2

The Impact of Adversarial Behavior at Work

The Consequences of Oppositional Behavior for Workplace Relationships

In this chapter we will examine in some detail what the implications are for a workplace that contains one or more adversarial colleagues, people who create relationships characterized by low levels of trust and support as well as some degree of personalized enmity. We will examine the dynamics found in working relationships in which there is little or no trust or support. Then we will explore the quality of relationships built by colleagues who are adversarial, before identifying a range of consequences that their behavior has for their colleagues, and indeed for themselves. The chapter will end with an opportunity for you to reflect on the character of your own adversarial colleagues and on any adversarial behavior you might have used yourself. However, let's start the chapter by discussing the ways in which adversarial colleagues are likely to employ political tactics and might also on occasional use bullying behavior.

ADVERSARIAL POLITICIANS, ADVERSARIAL BULLIES

I have written previously on the widespread challenge of handling political behavior in the workplace in *Managing Politics at Work: The Essential Toolkit for Identifying and Handling Political Behaviour in the Workplace* (2009). I have also written on the dynamics of responding effectively to bullying behavior in the workplace in *Managing Workplace Bullying: How to Identify, Respond to and Manage Bullying Behaviour in the Workplace* (2009). Let's now take a few moments to outline the differences and similarities between political, bullying, and adversarial behavior, before examining the ways in which adversarial co-workers can employ political or bullying tactics as they engage with their peers, team members, and managers. I have adapted the following material from *Managing Politics at Work* (2009) and *Managing Workplace Bullying* (2009), both of which are published by Palgrave Macmillan.

The essential differences between political, bullying and adversarial behaviors are as follows:

- Political behavior is about the degree to which a person's workplace activity is directed towards meeting their own internal agenda to acquire, for instance, greater power or kudos or control in the workplace, as opposed to working towards the goals associated with their role. The person using political behavior does so *without being transparent and open about what they want or what they are doing.* Some people only do things in political ways. Others use political tactics as and when they see the need to, or as self-protective strategies against other, more ruthlessly political colleagues. Political activity can be baffling to deal with in the workplace especially if you are not politically minded and go to work simply to do as good a job as you can. However, most people at work will use political behavior at some time in their lives, and in some organizations having a suitably developed suite of political tactics and political management skills is essential to being able to get things done.
- Bullying behavior is about a personalized, sustained attack on one colleague by another colleague using behaviors that are emotionally and psychologically punishing. The person responsible for using bullying behavior introduces a dynamic into a workplace relationship that involves a purposed attempt by them to injure their colleague's self-esteem, self-confidence, and reputation or to undermine their competence to carry out their work duties effectively. A campaign of bullying is characterized by the colleague using bullying behavior choosing to handle their relationship with the co-worker they target in a way that involves *removing power from that colleague and placing it with themselves.* Workplace bullying constitutes a deliberate, purposed attack on a colleague over weeks, months and sometimes years, based on the erroneous perception in the mind of the bully that they are justified in targeting that particular colleague. Sadly, reported incidents of workplace bullying are on the rise.
- Adversarial behavior is about one colleague behaving in ways that erode levels of support and trust in their working relationships while

also introducing a level of personalized enmity into their dealings with their co-workers. However, the aim of the adversarial colleague is not necessarily to injure their co-worker in a sustained attack, as with bullying behavior. Nor is it necessarily to acquire power or control or kudos, as with political behavior. Rather, it is more that the adversarial colleague prefers to introduce an element of antagonism into their relationships and has a preference for operating with low levels of trust and support for one very specific reason. It's so that they can keep their relationships loose and ill defined to avoid the possibility of being let down by placing themselves, as they see it, at risk. They are comfortable doing things this way, and prefer their colleagues to adjust to their values, whether or not this way of working comes naturally to them or results in effective outcomes. In this sense, adversarial colleagues place their personal need to devise loose and ill-defined relationships above their responsibility to build mutually effective workplace relationships.

What are the links between adversarial, bullying and political behavior? It is highly likely that every adversarial colleague will use political behavior of one kind or another at some point in their workplace relationships. The behavior they use will lack transparency and will result in lowered levels of trust in their relationships. However, it is not true to say that all users of political behavior at work are necessarily adversarial people. Many people who are not adversarial in intent do employ political behavior because in their workplaces it is the only way to get things done. Equally, while not all adversarial colleagues use bullying behavior, some of them might from time to time employ methods that involve using unjustified aggression against a particular co-worker. That is not to say that they *become workplace bullies*, as to do so they would need to specifically target one colleague in a sustained attack, but it does mean that the methods they choose at these times are characterized by bullying conduct.

So as far as our current discussion about adversarial colleagues goes, the state of affairs is one in which an adversarial colleague:

- May or may not use bullying behavior from time to time.
- Is highly likely to employ political strategies on a regular basis.

What impact do adversarial colleagues have in workplaces in which they are specifically employed to form effective working relationships with you and produce effective work in tandem with you?

THE DYNAMICS CREATED BY AN ADVERSARIAL COLLEAGUE

As previously noted, adversarial colleagues prefer to keep the boundaries of their working relationship with you loose and ill-defined. They like the room for maneuver this approaches gives them and the fact that it creates opportunities for them to wrongfoot you and keep you off balance. They want to do things this way because they can find the commitment to maintaining trust in a workplace relationship onerous and the responsibility required in relationships marked by a degree of supportiveness stifling.

Adversarial colleagues are unlikely to be transparent in their dealings with you. Providing only a limited degree of transparency, they can create dynamics that prove to be both confusing and unproductive for you to work with. You may work with adversarial colleagues who say 'teamwork matters,' but who, when you approach them for input, subsequently use behavior that signals 'don't expect any support from me.' You may have colleagues who go one step further and offer to provide you with input, but when you later take them up on the offer you may find that it is no longer available. Adversarial colleagues may or may not realize how challenging this approach can be for you to deal with. But on being given the feedback by you that it is awkward to be handled in this way, few will spontaneously alter their approach.

Their tendency to use behavior that erodes or precludes the formation of trust, while also being unsupportive, can create certain specific dynamics in their working relationship with you. These dynamics could include a tendency to:

- Provoke disputes which you don't want or see the need for, and which don't clarify any of the issues under debate.
- Sponsor turf wars and territorial arguments as they vie for influence with you.
- Endorse unhealthy competition between you and your other colleagues, competition which hinders progress and causes factions based on personalities to form within the workplace.
- Promote situations in which issues are not resolved, questions are not clarified, and suggestions are not progressed so that they can keep some room for maneuver around the workplace concerns that matter most to them.

Many adversarial colleagues have trouble with both commitment and responsibility inside workplace relationships. They may well work long hours and therefore may be widely regarded as employees who demonstrate considerable commitment to their employer. But spending a long time at work each day is quite different from having the integrity to say what you mean and mean what you say, and it is different again from taking responsibility for the impact of unhelpful behavior on colleagues. Adversarial colleagues rarely do either of these things, and consequently they can create dynamics at work which are draining for their co-workers to deal with. They can become adept at:

- Ignoring feedback on their behavior or only addressing it cursorily so that they don't have to amend their ways or address the intra-personal issues that result in them using an adversarial approach.
- Turning the tables on you should you complain about them or their conduct, making the issues you are complaining about your fault even though the genesis of these issues actually sits with them.
- Forming fragile alliances with you and some of their other co-workers, alliances that result in certain people coming together to achieve specific aims but which, once those aims have been attained, subsequently splinter and fragment.
- Maintaining unclear boundaries around their work responsibilities, boundaries that cause confusion for you, as you remain unsure about where the adversarial colleague considers their authority to start and where they consider it to end. You could be surprised by the level of emotion you have to deal with should you unwittingly step over an invisible line and stray into territory your adversarial colleague considers to belong to them.

Handling things in these ways will result in adversarial colleagues forming relationships at work which are characterized by certain specific features. Let's take a look at some of them.

THE QUALITY OF RELATIONSHIPS CREATED BY ADVERSARIAL BEHAVIOR

The basic issue facing those of you who work with adversarial colleagues is that they will be reluctant to build trust with you or to act in supportive ways towards you. They won't value your offering them support either. The relationship they build with you is likely to be characterized by:

- Little real listening.

- A tendency to make statements to you without really hearing what you are saying in return.
- An inclination to address solely their own concerns in meetings with you rather than to pay equal attention to your points of view, your agenda, or the issues you choose to put to them.
- An ability to create fog around issues and obfuscate when they consider it advantageous to do so.
- A propensity to become irrelevant when they want to avoid discussing an issue.
- A preference for covering up their perceived weaknesses or mistakes when dealing with you, a characteristic which may in turn make it difficult for you to admit any uncertainty or error to them.
- A tendency to resist or oppose suggestions from you about how they might improve their processes, work, or handling of certain issues.
- A propensity to become defensive should you want to make changes to work processes or schedules which they feel would rock the boat.
- A preference for creating 'no go issues' surrounding tasks for which they have primary responsibility and which they simply will not discuss with you, even if it is clear that you have some improvements to suggest or would value a discussion about the key issues.

Every adversarial colleague will have their own way of doing things and create a unique quality to their workplace relationships. You may well be able to add to this list, which is not intended to be exhaustive. But the key point here is that, from their own perspective, the behavior of the adversarial colleague makes complete sense to them, is comfortable for them, and keeps their relationships within territory that they like, territory characterized by little room for trust, supportive intent, or collegiality. However, it also creates dynamics at work that can preclude high-quality work being done and which are counter-intuitive, unproductive, and difficult for you and other people to handle. Very often, despite the difficulties they create and are responsible for, it will be *you* who ends up using adapted behavior on a regular basis just so that you can cope with the demands of your adversarial colleague's way of handling their workplace affairs. Let's establish these principles with an example.

CASE STUDY 3: ANSWERING THE QUESTION

A secondary school teacher is asked by the school head to run an intraschool project. He will work jointly with four other teachers on ways in which to improve the image of the school in the local community. The secondary school teacher is the most senior of the five teachers on the project. He does some preliminary thinking, and without soliciting input from anyone else on the team, circulates a series of bullet point suggestions about the way forward for the project to the other teachers on the team via email. The tenor of the email suggests that the secondary school teacher has firm ideas about the way the project should be handled, its aims and objectives, and he is surprised when one of his colleagues, a history teacher, replies to his email with a list of questions.

There are a number of ways in which the secondary school teacher could respond to the history teacher's email. Let's explore three of them:

- The secondary school teacher reads through the list of questions and replies on email to each one. His replies are sometimes quite lengthy and on other occasions quite brief. He determines the length of his reply based on his sense of the importance of the issue being raised by the history teacher and on his own interest in it.
- The secondary school teacher reads the list of questions. He thinks that some of them are good points and worth further debate, but he is disinclined to spend time responding to them. He sends the history teacher a reply saying that she has raised some good points and that he'd like to discuss them at the next project team meeting. He then circulates the entire list of questions to the other project team members along with the date and time of the next meeting.
- The secondary school teacher reads the questions with increasing annoyance. He waits five days and then responds to the history teacher with an email of his own. His replies are minimal, written in capital letters and convey an increasing sense of irritation to the history teacher. Two of his replies consist of one-word answers. The history teacher reads the email with dismay and interprets it as a clear sign that her input is not required.

Answering the Question: Analyzing the Dynamics

Let's revisit this situation to analyze the dynamics and explore the motivation of the secondary school teacher so that we can understand what his replies tell us about his nature.

In this example a secondary school teacher unilaterally decides how he would like to run a joint project and tells the other four people on the team about the conclusions he has come to. Having read his email a history teacher working on a project team decides to raise a number of issues with the team leader. She sends him an email. To her mind, the history teacher's actions demonstrate her enthusiasm for the project as well as her willingness to grapple at a deep level with the issues. She hopes that the team leader will receive her responses accordingly, and that she will be able to play an active role in determining the future direction of the project.

Let's now analyze the way in which the secondary school teacher running the project handles her questions to see what we can learn about his nature and the way in which he wants to manage his relationship with her.

- In the first instance, the secondary school teacher welcomes the history teacher's input. He reads her email carefully and responds to it in a timely and serious fashion. He answers each of her questions, paying more attention to some of them than to others. He demonstrates to her that he is open to her input, hears it, and will make judgments about what importance he attaches to the various points she raises. He does not take her email as a slight on his judgment or as a sign that she is straying into territory he considers to be uniquely his. Rather, his behavior makes it clear that, in this instance with this teacher, he is acting in an open and collaborative way, one that is consistent with a non-adversarial approach to building workplace relationships.
- In the second instance, the secondary school teacher reads the email from the history teacher but decides not to answer it himself. He can't really be bothered to address the issues that his colleague has raised, but recognizing that he cannot ignore them either, he decides that he will let the team handle them together rather than address them himself. He forwards the history teacher's email to the other members of the project team and sets the date and time for the next meeting. The team leader is overworked and a bit lazy, and doesn't want to do more than he has to in order to make the project a success. Not irresponsible enough to sideline the contents of the email completely, and not conscientious enough to answer its points himself, he ascribes responsibility for addressing its concerns to the entire project team. He doesn't actually like the history teacher's, as he sees it, overly conscientious approach to her role on the team. This is not because he is territorial or unwilling to accommodate her ideas, but because he wants to do

as little as possible and get away with this approach for as long as possible. He handles her email in a way that makes room for her input but which does not result in extra work for him. His lazy behavior makes it clear that while, in this instance, the secondary school teacher is going through the motions and is not being wholly uncooperative, neither is he adversarial.

In the third instance, the secondary school teacher is not at all pleased to be sent what he regards as an intrusive and unsolicited email from an interfering member of the team. He is especially displeased that the email appears, to his mind, to question his judgment by raising so many issues about the future direction of a project he is in charge of. He does not regard the mail as evidence of a conscientious co-worker. Rather it engages the adversarial side to him, a side which quickly acts in opposition to the history teacher. First, he does not reply to her email for five days. This is not because he is too busy to get to it, but because he wants her to have to wait for a reply so he can send her the message that responding to her input is something he would rather not have to do. Secondly, he sends back cursory and incomplete responses to every question that the history teacher raises, some of which are literally one word long, and all of which are written in capital letters. This is a ploy that, to his mind, denotes he is shouting at her on email, but whether she will regard it as evidence of ire or simply as evidence of an idiosyncratic typing style remains to be seen. His reply is calculated to reduce the history teacher and her input to unimportant and irritating, giving her the clear message that he hasn't got time for her or the issues she wants to raise. It is evidence that the secondary school teacher is acting in an adversarial fashion towards the history teacher, one that involves him in appearing uninterested in her input simply so that he can dissuade her from providing such input in future. The secondary school teacher would much rather that the history teacher and all the other members of the project team simply take his direction without debate or discussion. This approach suits him much better than active dialogue as it obviates the need for him to build working relationships with any of them, and means that he doesn't have to build some level of either trust or support with any of them. The history teacher now has a clear choice: try to get the secondary school teacher to re-engage with the issues she wants to raise with the project team and risk a more wrathful response from him, or play it his way and miss out on, as she sees it, an ideal opportunity to influence the way the school is regarded in the community.

Having spent some time analyzing the characteristics of working relationships in which one colleague is adversarial in nature, let's now explore the challenge before those of you who have to work day in, day out with such a colleague.

THE CHALLENGE OF WORKING WITH AN ADVERSARIAL COLLEAGUE

Those of you who recognize the adversarial dynamics described in this chapter from your own workplace experience need to learn to work effectively within these constraints. You need to find ways of building productive and effective relationships with colleagues who are:

- Not cooperative or accommodating.
- Not motivated by goodwill.
- Unlikely to respond innocently to gestures of openness.
- Not minded to value trust in relationships.
- Blind to the benefits of establishing mutually supportive connections at work.

Those of you who are basically non-adversarial in nature will most likely spontaneously use behavior which is to some degree or another open, collaborative, trusting and supportive. Those of you who see yourselves as predominantly using these kinds of non-adversarial behaviors can find that using this approach with an adversarial colleague is actually unwise. You can find that it doesn't build you influence with your adversarial colleague. Rather it can get you into trouble, losing you both personal power and respect. Rather than facilitate effective workplace contact with your adversarial colleague, using open and trusting behavior with them can backfire on you badly as they take advantage of your, as they see it, naivety and lack of wisdom in leaving yourself vulnerable to attack.

Those of you work in roles where you need to get things done in tandem with others in order to be effective may find that some or most of your key colleagues use similar open, collaborative styles to you. You probably find these co-workers straightforward and reasonable people to work with, and while you may not always agree with their points of view or their decisions, you can at least talk with them about the issues over which you hold alternative perspectives and agree to differ without falling out or becoming enemies.

But you may also work with adversarial colleagues with whom you share very little, colleagues who are neither open nor collaborative, and who do things in a very different way to you. These colleagues may not be supportive or approachable, and may not make themselves available for input when you need it. They may not use transparent or productive behavior often or at all. They may not value these ways of doing things, and in fact, may secretly think them a waste of time or derisory. Instead, their intent may be to make personalized attacks, however subtly delivered, on selected colleagues and on you, undermining those of you who are actively trying to get things done and reducing the likelihood of your continuing to invest in building productive, supportive, trusting relationships with them.

Some of you may have only one working contact that does things in this way. Others of you may find that the majority of your co-workers handle their workplace relationships like this. Sadly, the adversarial colleagues with whom you have to work closely can:

■ Reduce the standard of the work you are able to achieve.
■ Sap your energy.
■ Weaken your resolve.
■ Demoralize your spirits.

THE CONSEQUENCES OF ADVERSARIAL WORKING ENVIRONMENTS

Faced with dynamics such as these, it is little wonder that working in an adversarial environment can undermine teamwork, result in lowered standards of work and negatively affect customer perceptions. In fact, when workplace relationships are routinely characterized by low levels of trust and low levels of support relationships, they necessarily become more about self-protection, mistrust and unilateralism than about effective collaboration. Those of you who recognize this description may find that you put your workplace effort into:

■ Avoiding making mistakes rather than striving to improve standards or achieve stretching goals.
■ Avoiding addressing the issues you need to address in case doing so rocks the boat or creates an unpleasant or unexpected conflict.

- Avoiding responsibility for challenging yourself to learn and achieve, preferring to do just enough to get by instead.
- Avoiding committing heavily to bringing about workplace success, preferring to coast and let others carry the strain where possible.

In an environment that is largely adversarial, standards will suffer. It is inevitable as you become:

- Unclear where the where the boundaries lie.
- Confused about where your workplace responsibilities begin and end.
- Less able to perform effectively.
- Less conscientious about serving customers.
- Convinced that it is in your best interests to put your effort into other areas of your life.

Nonetheless, having to work inside adversarial relationships is likely to be the reality for many of you reading this book, and it is one with which you need to come to terms if you are to perform effectively in your role. Let's examine some of the options for doing so in an example.

CASE STUDY 4: ALTERED AGENDA

A member of a small risk assessment team in a niche brokerage house writes a monthly report on market sentiment and sends it to her peer for comment before distributing it round the office. Usually her peer suggests changes or makes suggestions on the .pdf before returning it to the risk assessor. She then decides what to incorporate and what to omit before circulating the final report. On this occasion her peer gets back to her on email saying that he has already sent out the report which he enjoyed. The risk assessor assumes that he had no comments to make and has saved her a task by circulating the report for her. Two days later she is dismayed to realize that the report has been changed in several places without her knowledge or her consent, and that in these places it no longer reflects her views. In fact the changes her peer has introduced mean that the report now contradicts her original opinion. She goes to his desk to discuss this unwelcome turn of events. She tells her peer that she thinks he has altered some of the wording in her report behind her back, and says that she wants to know what has happened and why. Her peer replies in a sneering tone by saying

'Behind your back! What is this? A kindergarten?' before walking swiftly towards the door of his office.

There are several ways in which the risk assessor could handle this situation. Let's examine three of them:

- Before he reaches the door of his office the risk assessor tells her peer that she is surprised by his conduct. She says that she hadn't thought he would be capable of acting in this way and wishes that he hadn't. Her peer shrugs his shoulders, and without breaking step, merely says 'Get past it' before walking through the doorway.
- Before he reaches the door of his office the risk assessor tells her peer that she is going to have to take this further. She is surprised to hear him reply in a nonchalant voice 'Do what you must' as he exists from his office.
- The risk assessor draws herself up to her full height and using a commanding voice tells her peer that she is quite clear what has happened. She informs him that her relationship with him has changed as a direct result of his decision to alter her report without her knowledge and to then circulate that report around the office. She informs him that she now clearly understands his character. She says that from now on she will do things in a different way as far as he is concerned. Her tone causes him to break step, and while she is still uttering her final few words, she walks smartly to the doorway and leaves the room before him.

Altered Agenda: Analyzing the Dynamics

Let's revisit this situation and analyze the dynamics in it so we can form a view as to which of these three ways of handling this challenging situation is most effective for the risk assessor.

In this example a risk assessor does what she has always done at work and hands over her monthly report to her peer for comment before she amends it and circulates it. Usually he returns the draft to her with his comments attached so that she can decide what to incorporate and what to amend or omit before sending out the final version of the report. But on this occasion, he doesn't return the report to her, and instead goes ahead and circulates it himself. He then gets back to his colleague and tells her that he has enjoyed the report and has already sent it out for her.

Two days later the risk assessor is horrified to realize that this isn't the whole story. While it is true that he has circulated the report, he has done so after having made a number of changes to the text, changes she had not sanctioned and of which she was unaware. In fact three of his changes now mean that the report says the opposite of what she wanted it to say. She decides that he has acted well outside of his authority and goes to talk to him. There is little doubt in her mind that he has deliberately acted against her by circulating a report that contradicts the point of view she wants to put across. Whether the report is actually now substandard or could be taken as evidence of sloppy thinking on her part remains to be seen. The changes may or may not cause trouble for her with her colleagues, and may or may not succeed in altering their good opinion of her. That is not the point as far as she is concerned. The point is that someone she has worked with in an established and effective way for some time has acted in a fashion that fundamentally alters the dynamic between them, and the risk assessor wants to get to the bottom of it.

She goes to his office. She asks him why he has altered some of the wording in her report behind her back. She has to suffer the ignominy of hearing him sneer at her, something he has not done before. He tells her that she is behaving as if she is in a kindergarten. In this one phrase the peer effectively turns the tables on his colleague, making her, as he puts it, childish perception of events the issue rather than his conduct. This is an amazing thing for the peer to say, given that it is he who is in the wrong, he who has acted in a reprehensible way. It is another clear piece of evidence, should she need it, that, whatever the character of her relationship with him up until this point, the risk assessor now needs to handle this colleague with particular caution. He has already proven himself capable of acting behind her back, and now compounds his offense by ridiculing her subsequent quite legitimate complaint.

Let's now analyze the dynamics and the consequences of the three different ways in which she could handle this evolving situation:

■ In the first instance, the risk assessor is astonished at the unexpected ferocity of her peer's caustic comment in which he compares her legitimate complaint to kindergarten behavior. Even though she is thrown, she tells her peer that she is surprised at his recent behavior and wishes he hadn't taken the actions he has taken. On the face of it these are sensible remarks to make. They express her feelings about what has happened as well as her regret, and they appear to be both assertive and straightforward points to make.

But they have no effect at all on her peer, who merely shrugs his shoulders and tells her to 'Get past it'. Why did the risk assessor's rebuke have no effect on her peer? It is because he doesn't care that she is upset. The whole tenor of her comments to him is that she is disappointed by his actions, which came out of the blue and which have resulted in her feeling betrayed by him. Nonetheless, he is unmoved. This peer does not have any concerns about his actions, even if the risk assessor does, and he doesn't think he was unwise to have taken them. So he doesn't care that the trust between them has been injured and that she is upset. Only time will tell how the rest of the office will react to him once the truth about his conduct is out, but for now, this peer is unconcerned about his actions and has no time for any disappointment that the risk assessor might feel in response to them. He shrugs her comments off as inconsequential to him and moves on, expecting her to do the same.

- In the second instance, the risk assessor summons up the strength to tell her peer that she is going to take things further. The implication is that she is going to make a complaint about him and let the office know what has happened. This also appears to be a strong response to duplicitous behavior. But, once more, it does not appear to strike home with the adversarial peer, whose reply is offhand and casual. Whether he really is as unconcerned as he appears to be when he utters the phrase 'Do what you must,' only he will know. But he certainly wants his peer to think he is relaxed about the situation. He walks out of his office apparently indifferent to the consequences for the risk assessor or himself of his actions, and leaves her feeling thwarted and let down. Once again she has failed to hold him accountable for his actions. Why? Because this is a man who is so enamored of his cleverness and political astuteness that he thinks he will get away with it whether the risk assessor makes a complaint or not. He believes that his well-used toolkit of obfuscating, scapegoating, and fogging tactics will serve him well should he have to give account for his conduct to anyone else in the office. He's been here before. He will be here again. How hard can it be? He doesn't feel concerned at the possible consequences her complaint might raise for him. He feels complacent. And his colleague is left frustrated and without an explanation for his apparently groundless change of heart towards her.

- In the third instance, however, the risk assessor does give her peer pause for thought. She doesn't complain to him, threaten him, and ask him to explain himself or suggest that he has acted poorly.

Instead she merely tells him what she will do as a direct result of his conduct. She informs him in a clear and commanding voice that her relationship with him has now changed and that she will do things differently from now on where he is concerned. She informs him that she now fully understands his character. Then, while she is still speaking, she demonstrates her altered approach by walking out of the door, leaving him standing there. This represents a significant change in values on her part. Previous to this encounter, she would not have ended a meeting so abruptly or so unilaterally. Now, though, the relationship is on a different footing and she has altered her approach to it accordingly. Her peer isn't expecting this turn of events. He has made the assumption that the risk assessor will be a relatively easy target for his adversarial maneuver, and he supposes wrongly. Rather than handle the situation ineffectively, she demonstrates sufficient strength and guile to leave him wondering what she might do next, and he is left rooted to the spot considering his options. He is unlikely to back down or apologize. But he might not try something like this again with her in future. For sure, their working relationship will remain tarnished by his actions, but the risk assessor has reduced the likelihood that her peer will repeat such an obviously adversarial tactic with her in the short term.

Successive chapters of this book will concentrate on exploring in depth how to respond effectively to adversarial behavior from peers, team members, and managers. It will also examine how to work with and alongside colleagues who use adversarial behavior selectively or intermittently. These chapters will expand on the descriptions of adversarial behaviors presented in these first two chapters of the book so that those of you for whom this way of doing things is unnatural, opaque, and at best something you regard as counter-productive, will stand a better chance of identifying it early on and handling it effectively when you next encounter it.

YOUR ADVERSARIAL COLLEAGUES

You may now like to take a moment to consider the character of the adversarial colleagues you work with. You can jot down your answers to the following questions in the spaces below each one:

■ What issues does the use of adversarial behavior in your workplace create for you at work?

■ In what ways do you think the quality of your work is affected by adversarial behavior in your workplace?

■ Identify one incident of adversarial behavior being employed by a colleague that adversely impacted your work. How did you respond at the time? What impact did this approach have on your colleague's subsequent behavior?

■ If you were in the same situation again, what would you change about the way you handled this incident of adversarial behavior?

■ Identify one specific situation in which you used adversarial behavior in the workplace. What factors caused you to employ these methods? What impact did your choice of behavior have on your colleagues at the time?

■ If you were in the same situation again, what would you change about your approach?

SUMMARY AND NEXT CHAPTER

This chapter has suggested that adversarial colleagues tend to create specific consequences for those who work alongside them, and that these outcomes are likely to be uncomfortable for you to deal with and unhelpful for the standards of work you produce. The chapter has highlighted that in order to be effective at handling an adversarial colleague, you would do well to employ specific tactics that simultaneously are self-defending and hold the adversarial colleague accountable for their actions. We will examine these tactics in more detail throughout the rest of the book.

The next chapter will examine in greater detail the key role of trust and support at work. It will highlight the links between trust and support, and illustrate how 'offering support' can mean different things to different colleagues. The chapter will suggest that the challenge posed by working alongside an adversarial colleague could prove draining and even damaging to those of you who don't find productive ways to handle their behavior and who don't succeed in finding adequate levels of support in your workplace.

CHAPTER 3

Low Trust, Low Support

The Cornerstones of an Adversarial Approach

In this chapter we will examine in some detail the importance of trust and support to workplace relationships. We will explore the decision to trust a colleague, the decision to offer support to a colleague, and the decision to receive support from a colleague. Then we will examine the links between the three things. We will explore how those of you who work in highly challenging environments may want or need more support than those of you who experience your work as less challenging. We will examine the difference between healthy and unhealthy challenge at work, and explore how adversarial colleagues represent an unhealthy, draining challenge to those of you who work alongside them regularly. The chapter will identify how 'being supportive' means different things to different people, highlighting how misunderstandings can occur when one colleague's expression of support may not be experienced by another as supportive. And we will examine how adversarial colleagues prefer to operate with little or no trust or support, and purposefully construct their relationships along these lines. The chapter will end by taking a look at your own experiences of working with non-adversarial colleagues whom you consider to be supportive and whom you trust, as well as your experiences of working with adversarial colleagues who you consider to be unsupportive and challenging to work with, and whom you do not trust.

THE ROLE OF TRUST AND SUPPORT AT WORK

Trust and support at work go together. They are two sides of the same workplace relational coin. You are very unlikely to support a colleague whom you do not trust, and as unlikely to trust a colleague who does not act supportively towards just you. Equally, while you may on occasion offer support to a colleague who does not act supportively towards you, it is more likely that you will reserve these offers for those co-workers with whom you have established mutually beneficial ways of getting things done. The trick is being able to make accurate judgments about what does and what does not constitute:

■ Supportive behavior.
■ Evidence of a trustworthy character.

When there are so many different ways to express either or both of these attributes, these are important judgment calls to get right.

I have written previously on the nature of trust at work in Chapter 10 of *Managing Politics at Work: The Essential Toolkit for Identifying and Handling Political Behaviour in the Workplace* (2009, Palgrave Macmillan, pp 130–47). The key points for our discussion here, which I have adapted from pages 138–9 of that book, are as follows:

■ The decision to trust a colleague is an individual choice based on evidence that you personally consider to be credible.
■ Only you can decide what constitutes compelling evidence for you of someone meriting your trust, but it may include your colleague establishing liking and respect with you, it may be related to the consistent quality of their job performance, or it may be a combination of both.
■ Whatever the nature of the evidence, it leads you to believe that, for the greater part, your colleague will handle things in ways that you like and with sufficient integrity that you will feel comfortable working with them.
■ This evidence also results in you feeling that your colleague will work consistently towards the goals and objectives associated with their role, and not adopt an adversarial, overly political, or bullying approach to working alongside you.
■ The evidence you consider credible is such that you believe it to be, by and large, predictive of your colleague's future behavior.

Some of you will make rapid, instinctual decisions about which of your colleagues is and which is not worthy of your trust. For you, the evidence you believe is your instinct about your colleague. Others of you may take your time and want to see repeated behavioral evidence of a person's values before you determine whether or not to extend trust to them, and over which issues to extend trust to them as well. To complicate matters further, you may find that some of your colleagues prove trustworthy in some areas of their working lives and relationship with you but not in others. In these cases your job is to make accurate distinctions about where these boundaries lie. One of the pieces of evidence that may prove influential to you is whether a colleague does or does not act supportively towards you.

THE LINKS BETWEEN SUPPORT AND CHALLENGE

Some of your workplace relationships will be characterized by a high degree of mutual support. Others will be marked by no supportive intent either way. There will be many that lie on different places on the continuum in between, places characterized by you giving or receiving support some of the time, and your colleagues doing likewise. To some degree, the extent to which you need support at work will be determined by the degree of challenge you experience in your work, and the degree to which you feel able to rise to that challenge without soliciting additional input.

Those of you who experience your work itself or your key workplace relationships as high on challenge may well want or need more support than those of you who experience these things as less challenging. Equally, as your workload and the character of your relationships changes, becoming less challenging or supportive for some periods of time and more so at other times, so your need for support will fluctuate too.

Your offers of support to colleagues may well be influenced by your perceptions about the degree of challenge in their workload and the degree to which you regard their key relationships as more or less onerous for them to handle. When working with non-adversarial co-workers there is little risk in offering support or accepting offers of support. Your colleague is unlikely to take advantage of you in either case, and the benefits of working in this way will usually outweigh the risks associated with the vulnerability. But that is not true when working with an adversarial colleague. In this instance any offer of support made by an adversarial colleague may well come with hidden strings, and any offer of support you make to them may be quickly regretted should your adversarial colleague try to take advantage of any room for maneuver that your openness gives them. We will shortly explore the nature of the challenge of working with an adversarial colleague in greater detail, but first let's explore the links between support and challenge in your day-to-day work.

SUPPORT AND CHALLENGE IN YOUR WORK

Consider the following framework. The framework asks you to step back from a particular piece of work and assess your situation on it from two simultaneous perspectives. These are the:

■ Degree of challenge you experience day-to-day as you think about the issues, execute against the tasks, and resolve the problems with which you are dealing.
■ Degree of support you receive day-to-day while handling this piece of work.

The framework is project driven. It is quite possible for you to place yourself in one category on one project, but in another category on a second project, depending on your view of the degree of challenge inherent in those two different sets of tasks and the differing degrees of support you receive from your colleagues while working on them. So identify a specific piece of work on which you are engaged, and determine where you place yourself in relation to that set of tasks on the framework shown in Figure 3.1.

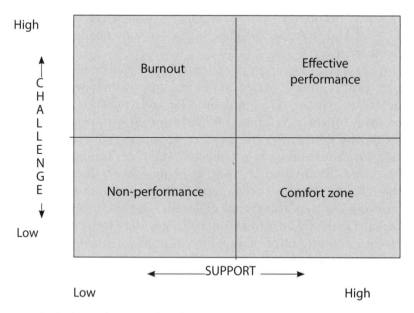

Figure 3.1 The links between challenge and support at work

Aryanne Oade (2010).

- Burnout: if you place yourself in the area of burnout you consider that your work on the project you have selected involves a degree of challenge not matched by the degree of support available to you. You think that the mismatch is such that you are in a burnout zone one which, if you don't find additional sources of meaningful support or if you don't succeed in lowering the level of day-to-day challenge in your work, may result in you running into trouble. You may expend your energy without achieving your goals and have to give account to your managers for your failure to deliver. Or you may dip into an area of physical or psychological distress. If this is the case you may experience a variety of stress-related symptoms such as having uncharacteristic difficulty making decisions, higher than usual levels of anxiety, less refreshing sleep, loss of appetite, or increased levels of irritation and tiredness.

- Non-performance: if you place yourself in the area of non-performance you are lacking a healthy degree of challenge in your work on this project. You are also without any or much effective support, although it would be true to say that you don't need that much. You characterize your current situation as one of inertia and stagnation. You think that the work you are doing is not stretching enough and the quality of dialogue that you have with your colleagues lacks stimulation, ideas or encouragement. You may also be experiencing increased levels of tiredness or irritation, and also have trouble motivating yourself simply because you are bored. You may want to consider what steps you could take to increase the degree of challenge that you face on a day-to-day basis so that you become more energized, as well as considering what you could do to increase the quality of support you experience in the workplace.

- Comfort zone: if you place yourself in the comfort zone you have sufficient support on this project but not enough challenge. For short periods of time, depending on what you look for from work, you may find this combination of factors enables you to recharge your batteries. But the likelihood is that longer periods of time spent working in this way will lead to you feeling comfortable but becoming ineffective. You might begin to feel frustrated and bored. You might find yourself putting less into this area of your work because of the lack of healthy challenge it entails. You may find yourself looking for stimulation elsewhere, and even decide that you would prefer to put the effort you normally put into a project into areas of your life away from the workplace. It is likely that, while you enjoy the people you work with on this project, there is too little momentum or stimulus in your day-to-day activities for you to find your labor satisfying.

■ Effective performance: if you place yourself in the area of effective performance then you are likely to experience your work on this project as stimulating and energizing. At times it may well tax you, perhaps too much on occasion, but overall the combination of stretching work and high levels of support is one you thrive on, one that brings the best out of you. You may well think that you are producing good results on this project, producing work that is high-quality and creative. Only you will know for how long a period of time you can maintain working at this pace without a break to recharge and assimilate, but for now, it seems to be working well for you.

THE CHALLENGE PRESENTED BY ADVERSARIAL COLLEAGUES

What is the connection between the discussion we have just been having about support and challenge and issues around working with adversarial colleagues? The key issue is that an adversarial colleague will inevitably create challenges for you to overcome as you work alongside them. It is in their nature. The challenge they ask you to overcome is not the usual healthy workplace requirement to:

■ Grapple with complex task-related issues and resolve them.
■ Find new and more creative ways of addressing customer requirements.
■ Endure under pressure and demonstrate active commitment to your work.

The challenges that an adversarial colleague is likely to present you with are about:

■ Them.
■ The quality of their relationship with you.
■ Their desire to be antithetical and oppositional towards you.
■ Their preference for establishing working relationships characterized by little or no trust and support.

An adversarial colleague will ask you to handle *their internal agenda* – to demonstrate lower than usual levels of commitment or responsibility and a degree of antipathy towards you – and, depending on how marked their oppositional streak is and how often you have contact with them, you may well be required to handle these things on a day-to-day basis *as well as* handle the normal challenges associated with your role.

Every workplace role has challenges pertaining to it, and depending on your character and constitution, work issues that you experience as challenging could be unremarkable to your colleagues. For instance, you may really dislike and find onerous the need to handle disappointed customers while another colleague may feel well equipped to do so. Equally, you may find it difficult initiating a new project while other colleagues, with different dispositions and temperaments, may enjoy this aspect of their work most of all. The same is true of adversarial colleagues. While there may be those of you who enjoy sparring with an adversarial colleague from time to time. there are probably fewer of you who enjoy doing so day in, day out while working on high-profile, engaging, and taxing projects.

Working alongside an adversarial colleague who expects you to cope with the interpersonal friction, irritations, dilemmas, and difficulties which they pose can be draining. Dealing with this set of circumstances over a prolonged period of time and with insufficient support can move even the most robust and effective performer towards the burnout zone. Even if you work with other supportive colleagues, having one strongly oppositional co-worker with whom you cannot avoid working can significantly add to your stress and to the unhelpful challenges you face at work.

It is inevitable that those of you who work day in, day out alongside adversarial colleagues who handle things in this provoking way, colleagues whose behavior precludes the usual levels of trust and support developing between you, will find it difficult to produce your best work. It is inevitable that you will, from time to time, find the stresses and strains placed upon you by your adversarial colleague's behavior onerous and energy-sapping. Those of you who find yourselves in this situation on a regular basis may well want or need higher than usual levels of support from your co-workers. In fact, one of the mitigating factors, which could make your relationship with a truly adversarial colleague easier to navigate, is having access to co-workers who are able to offer you meaningful support.

DIFFERENT PEOPLE, DIFFERENT EXPRESSIONS OF SUPPORT

The problem is that actions that any particular colleague experiences as supportive, and which they might be minded to replicate when offering support to you, may not be experienced by you as helpful. Consider the following short examples:

- A busy accountant is detail conscious, precise, and thoughtful. She likes to understand a situation fully before acting, and on occasions where she needs support from her boss, wants him to help her see the wood from the trees. Unfortunately for her, his style emphasizes generating momentum and the big picture. She would like him to sit down with her, talk her through her workload, help her prioritize her tasks, and provide her with helpful structure. But she finds his quick mind, probing questions, and attempts to direct her work brash, impractical, and overwhelming. Her boss is confused by her reaction to his attempts to mentor her, as he genuinely wants to be helpful, and while he realizes that he isn't being, doesn't know why.

- An inexperienced schoolteacher is an empathic listener. She easily builds rapport with her colleagues and is a reliable and effective performer. Her interpretation of receiving support is to be listened to. She finds active listening particularly helpful, and needs her colleagues to ask her insightful questions that will enable her to find her own answers. She experiences her confident and task-focused peer as particularly overbearing, and can even feel inadequate around him when he good-naturedly asks her how it is going. Her uncomfortable, short replies to his well-intended questions leave him feeling awkward and slightly embarrassed.

- A media consultant is outgoing, politically astute and flexible. He is adept at marketing achievements and managing perceptions. What he means by support is having a senior colleague who will notice when things go well for him and publicize the fact, who will provide him with the resources he needs to carry on with his work, and who will reward him for reaching his goals. But his boss uses a much more structured and ordered style than he does, one that emphasizes thoroughness and planning, and one in which he anticipates and talks about how to manage possible upcoming risks. The media consultant experiences his boss's attempts to support him as annoying. He complains that they slow him down, curb his enthusiasm, and bog him down in unwanted details and questions. His boss is surprised and disappointed, as he wants to be supportive and feels thwarted that he does not know how to engage effectively with this particular team member.

You may like to spend a few minutes considering what constitutes effective workplace support for you. You can answer the following questions and jot down your responses to them in the space below each one:

■ Identify a colleague whom you experience as particularly supportive. What does this person do or say that you find helpful?

■ Identify a colleague whom you experience as particularly unsupportive. What does this person do or say that you find unhelpful?

■ Should you find yourself needing support to help mitigate the impact of an adversarial co-worker, what would be most helpful to you? Who might you approach for such input? How will you go about approaching them?

Let's now establish the principles we have been discussing in this chapter in more detail, using a longer example set in the world of fashion magazines.

CASE STUDY 5: WORKING WITHOUT TRUST

A fashion magazine editor approaches a journalist who is both a writer and a photographer. The journalist is just starting her freelance career, and the editor telephones her to ask her to take a series of images of street wear and write a piece about changing trends on the high street. The journalist is pleased to be approached, and accepts the commission, which will mean working with an editor she has not yet met or worked with. During her first telephone conversation with the editor, the journalist becomes concerned at the way the conversation is going. She picks up on the peremptory manner of the editor, and forms the view that she is could be tricky to work with. During the first call the editor twice refers to herself as 'the expert.' The journalist's instincts tell her that the editor has a high need for control and doesn't listen very effectively. The editor twice avoids answering points the journalist puts to her, ignoring them in preference for addressing other points of her own choosing. In their second call the journalist, who is very detail conscious, makes a point of saying that she would like to run through the ins and outs of the assignment again so that she can be sure that the two of them have the same view of the scope and overall goal of the project. The journalist is amazed when the editor interrupts her to inform her in a high-handed manner that 'publishing is all about details' before promptly ringing off.

Working Without Trust: Analyzing the Dynamics

Let's revisit this scenario to analyze the dynamics and explore the ins and outs of the situation. In it a magazine editor approaches a journalist and hires her to do a piece of work. During their initial telephone call the journalist realizes that the editor might be tricky to deal with. Her instincts tell her this, as does the editor's behavior when she deliberately ignores points put to her by the journalist on two separate occasions. Towards the end of the second call, when the journalist decides to clarify the scope and detail of the project just to be on the safe side, she is amazed when the editor unilaterally ends the call with the withering words 'publishing is all about details' without answering her question about what the details are. What can we glean from the editor's behavior about her mindset, her trustworthiness, and her intent towards the journalist?

The editor displays a number of adversarial traits in her dealings with the journalist. She does not approach either telephone call in a collaborative way. Nor does she seek to cooperate with the journalist as they discuss the project and the way it might go. Rather, from their first conversation, the editor tries to gain the upper hand, referring to herself as 'the expert' and attempting to cow the journalist into complying with her will. She doesn't succeed, and in fact does such a good job of alerting the journalist to her ambivalent nature that the journalist decides to make sure of her ground.

The journalist suggests that it would be useful for the two of them to clarify the detail and the parameters of the project. She decides to do this because, being both detail conscious and meticulous, she wants to make sure that she and the editor will be singing from the same hymn sheet. Her request is perfectly reasonable, but the response of the editor is not. She seizes the moment and goes onto the offensive. Her authoritative snap that 'publishing is all about details,' coupled with her decision to hang up without another word, conveys to her new colleague all she needs to know. This one action confirms the journalist's suspicions, and creates sufficient concern in her mind that she will do well to think twice about continuing with the project. She realizes the following:

- First, the editor is skilled at turning the tables on her. She is willing to use the journalist's innocent and reasonable request as a pretext for behaving in a commanding way. As soon as the journalist suggests that she and the editor review the parameters of the project, in other words as soon as the journalist suggests that the two of them work together on something important, the editor pounces. In one simple phrase she changes the dynamic in the conversation, and therefore the relationship, from a suggestion that the two of them work together into a ruthless put-down that at once undermines the journalist, reduces her concerns to nothing, and leaves her confused about the scope of the work.

- Second, the editor reacts to, as she hears it, the suggestion that the journalist might need some support with ruthlessly efficiency. She regards what she sees as 'needing support at work' as a weakness, and jumps at the chance to demonstrate to the journalist that not only is she above all that, but she has no time for such failings in others. In fact she regards the journalist's quite understandable wish to work with her to define the scope of the project as an ugly vulnerability, an unacceptable flaw in her character, and one that she will not tolerate.

- The editor deliberately fails to address the journalist's concerns about the scope and details of the project so that, at some later date when it suits her, she can slap the journalist down, attacking her for, perhaps, having misunderstood the essentials of the project and gone off down the wrong route, or having failed to produce a piece of work that is to specification.

- ■ The editor takes these actions to convey in clear and unassailable terms to her, as she sees it, more junior colleague that she is in charge. She is trying to pave the way for the adversarial dynamic she wishes to introduce into the relationship, one that leaves issues unresolved and the boundaries of tasks vague so that she can attack, reduce, or undermine the competence of her colleague as and when she chooses in future.

She may or may not consistently behave in this fashion. But, these actions have the effect of precluding any trust from forming in the early stages of the relationship between the editor and the journalist. For the editor, this is fine. She doesn't value trust and doesn't care whether or not the journalist trusts her. But to the journalist, who is not an adversarial character, this is a difficult and confusing state of affairs. She actually performs better when she is working with a supportive and interested colleague. In this case, she can be in no doubt that the editor will not be available for input, will offer her little or no effective support, could prove to be consistently untrustworthy, and will certainly be challenging to work with for all the wrong reasons.

The journalist worries that, working within these constraints, not only will she not enjoy the work as much as she might had she been working with someone more amenable, but she will not do her best work either. She worries that, whichever category she places herself in at the start of the project, she will inevitably move towards the burnout zone, propelled there under the pressures of working for this adversarial editor. She knows that, for her, the quality of the relationships she builds with her colleagues affects the quality of the work she subsequently is able to produce. She is concerned that working with this editor will prove a disabling experience for her, not only because she cannot now be sure what the parameters of the project are, but also because she will have no one to go to should she want to bounce ideas around or seek clarification about something. Instead, she will be working with an editor who is a formidable foe and one quite capable of delivering a devastating, one-line put-down out of the blue.

Only the journalist will be able to determine whether or not she wants to work with such an editor, although at such an early stage in her freelance career, it will be difficult for her to turn down such a high-profile piece of work.

YOUR ADVERSARIAL COLLEAGUES

You might now like to apply the material from this chapter to your own working relationships. You can answer the following questions and jot down your answers to each of them in the space below it:

■ Identify a colleague whom you regard as being both supportive and trustworthy, at least in some matters. What specific things does this colleague say or do which lead you to regard them in this light?

■ What impact does this combination of supportive and trustworthy characteristics have on you and your work?

■ Identify a colleague whom you regard as being unsupportive and untrustworthy. What specific things does that colleague say or do which lead you to regard them as being unsupportive and untrustworthy?

■ What impact does this combination of unsupportive and untrustworthy characteristics have on you and your work?

■　What steps can you take in future to mitigate the risks associated with working with this colleague?

SUMMARY AND NEXT CHAPTER

This chapter has suggested that trust and support are two sides of the same workplace relational coin, and that rarely does one of these things exist in a working relationship apart from the other. It has highlighted the fact that some healthy challenge is needed at work to stimulate you towards effective performance, but that the challenge posed by an adversarial co-worker is often unhealthy, counter-productive, and draining. The chapter has illustrated how different people offer support in different ways, and that one colleague's expression of supportive intent may not be experienced as supportive by the colleague to whom they offer it.

The chapter has highlighted how finding effective sources of support is important for those of you who work with adversarial co-workers. It closed with an example that illustrated how adversarial colleagues act in unsupportive and untrustworthy ways, and included opportunities for you to apply its material to your working life.

The next chapter focuses on the issues involved in working with a colleague who sometimes uses adversarial behavior and who sometimes doesn't. Rather than always acting in an oppositional and ambivalent way these colleagues can be collegial and can use open and productive behavior on a regular basis. These circumstances make it all the more surprising therefore when they start to use an alternative approach, one characterized by adversarial behavior, even with those colleagues with whom they have, up until that moment, enjoyed positive working relationships. The chapter will examine the circumstances in which such colleagues may change their approach from largely or completely non-adversarial to adversarial, and offers insights into what situational and intrapersonal factors that might cause them to do so.

CHAPTER 4

Selective Adversarial Behavior

Colleagues who Sometimes Use an Adversarial Approach and who Sometimes Don't

Not every colleague who uses an adversarial approach will do so on a continual basis. While some colleagues may use adversarial behavior all the time and have no other way of doing things, others employ adversarial methods as and when they feel the need to rather than constantly. Their strategy is to adopt a selectively oppositional approach with certain colleagues only over certain issues. And it can be confusing to say the least for those of you who have, up until the change of tack, enjoyed an effective and cordial working relationship with a colleague to find that your erstwhile pleasant co-worker is now your adversarial-minded foe.

This chapter addresses the issue of selective adversarial behavior: behavior which can *appear* to come out of the blue but for which there is always a reason, even if it is opaque to onlookers and only clear in the mind of the colleague whose behavior has altered. The chapter will highlight what situational factors and what intrapersonal factors can cause an otherwise non-adversarial colleague to use adversarial behavior from time to time, or with selected colleagues only. It will illustrate these principles with some clear examples, and encourage you to reflect on your own workplace experiences of working with or alongside selective adversarial colleagues, and of using selective adversarial behavior yourself.

THE DECISION TO USE SELECTIVE ADVERSARIAL BEHAVIOR

From time to time almost everyone at work uses competitive, spirited behavior. An issue arises about which you feel strongly, and you set about ensuring that your voice is heard, your preferred outcome is achieved, and that those who oppose you fail. Usually you will select this approach when the issues involved are so important or pressing that you can see no way forward other than your chosen outcome. So you use behavior that makes it clear that you will have no truck with opposition and will expect people to get out of your way so that you can bring about the outcome to which you are committed.

Let's make a distinction between this quite common way of handling certain workplace issues and selective adversarial behavior. Selective adversarial behavior might appear superficially similar to the competitive approach described above. But a closer look reveals that it is not. A selectively adversarial colleague, one who moves into an occasional or infrequent adversarial mindset, may well use methods that come across as competitive, but the key difference is that they select them not because they want to prevail on a certain *issue* that is important to them, but because they have come to regard a particular colleague as their *enemy*. Consider the following short examples:

- A head teacher hears his deputy head's suggestion, voiced for the first time at a governors meeting, that the school needs to offer a greater choice of extra-curricular activities as a direct threat to his authority, and roundly slaps him down. From that moment onwards – but only immediately before, during and after governors meetings – the head teacher employs adversarial methods in his dealings with the deputy head. He remains non-adversarial in his dealings with his number two on all other occasions, and does not use these methods with any other member of his staff.
- A trading desk head decides that to save time she will approach one of her peer's team members without informing him in advance. However, this action inadvertently changes the nature of her previously cordial working relationship with her peer. From that moment onwards he regards her with mistrust and employs selectively adversarial tactics with her. He perceives her as someone who has crossed a boundary that she ought not to have crossed, and decides that, as a consequence, she has become a potential business foe. He starts to employ adversarial methods in his dealings with her, but only in his one-to-one encounters with her. When in the presence of other colleagues, he treats her with the same degree of professional courtesy as all his other colleagues.
- A hospital accountant decides to use adversarial behavior with one of his team members after she takes on a new project without

checking it out with him first. In retaliation, he denies her routine information, information that he disseminates freely to everyone else in the team. He continues to use these tactics with her until he notices a discernible change in her demeanor towards him, a change that he interprets as a sign of her renewed submission to his authority, whereupon he reduces the intensity of his adversarial tactics. However, every now and then, to show her that he is watching her like a hawk and hasn't forgotten that she is capable of getting it wrong, the accountant employs an adversarial behavior in his dealings with her simply to keep her on her toes.

THE IMPACT OF SELECTIVE ADVERSARIAL BEHAVIOR

The problem for those of you who observe selective adversarial behavior in one of your otherwise largely non-adversarial colleagues is that you might not know what has caused your colleague to alter their approach. You may or may not be close enough to the action that precedes a particular change of heart to understand what specific circumstances irk your colleague in what particular way, and what specific circumstances subsequently cause them to relent. It can be unsettling to witness a once cordial working relationship between two co-workers descend into adversarial strife, because it will inevitably raise a question in your mind about whether or not you might also incur the wrath of your colleague at some future date and also be subject to adversarial behavior. And it can be challenging and confusing to say the least if you are unfortunate enough to be the person who is singled out for adversarial methods by a colleague with whom you had previously enjoyed an effective working relationship. You may genuinely not understand what actions you took or what words you used that caused your colleague to turn on you.

So what factors could account for a normally non-adversarial colleague choosing to employ adversarial behavior? Consider the following example, which is set in a hospital pharmacy.

CASE STUDY 6: CHANGE OF HEART

Two pharmacists jointly manage a busy hospital dispensary. They work well together, making shared decisions about all aspects of the pharmacy's work including stock ranges and levels, opening hours and staff-related issues. The two pharmacists have broadly similar styles and relatively similar levels of experience. There is no competition or rivalry between them, and when they disagree, which is relatively infrequently, they find a way to resolve their issues by talking them through. Their manager recognizes how effectively they work together and allows them room to do so. He keeps in touch with them on a weekly basis and trusts them to approach him outside of their Friday morning meeting should they need to. This arrangement works well, and the three people comment that they enjoy working together.

However, when their trusting and hands-off boss retires and is replaced by a younger and more hands-on manager, neither of the pharmacists likes their new boss's style. They object to his unexpected visits and direct questioning. They dislike the fact that he seems to expect them to stop their work and give him their full attention as soon as he arrives unannounced. They complain to one another about his slightly peremptory manner, and agree that they would prefer it if their old boss came back.

After two weeks of the new regime one of the pharmacists notices that her colleague seems unusually withdrawn and uncommunicative towards her, and wonders if she is ill. From that moment onwards she experiences an increasing change in her colleague's attitude and behavior towards her. Rather than share information with her in an easy and straightforward way as she would usually do, this second peer becomes slightly secretive. On various occasions she claims that she has mislaid paperwork that she would normally talk through with her colleague, and on other occasions she arranges update meetings with her boss at times when she knows her colleague will be at lunch.

While continuing to comment warmly about how effectively she and her colleague work together this second peer starts to work against her in smaller and larger ways. She speaks with their staff members when her peer is occupied, and fails to inform her about the conversations on her return. She orders stock from different suppliers without discussing this development with her colleague. She starts to make slighting and undermining comments about her peer to their boss out of earshot of her co-worker. Eventually, after making several increasingly derogatory remarks about her peer to their joint manager, she arranges a one-to-one meeting with him and suggests to him that her colleague is not really up to the job of managing the pharmacy and is being carried by her. She ends the meeting by suggesting that he ought to promote her to run the pharmacy single-handedly so that he can leave her to get on with it and have more time available for managing upwards.

Change of Heart: Analyzing the Dynamics

Let's revisit this situation to analyze the dynamics in it and explore the motivation of the second peer. We will examine her conduct to identify what factors result in her change of attitude and behavior towards a colleague with whom she has previously worked so well.

In this example a hospital dispensary is jointly run by two pharmacists who do a good job of dividing up their responsibilities. They establish and maintain a cordial and effective partnership and enjoy working for a manager who trusts them to carry out their joint duties effectively. However, when their long-standing manager is replaced by a more engaged and actively involved manager whose style does not sit comfortably with either pharmacist, their relationship suffers. One of the two pharmacists feels the need to handle her peer differently, and she is tricky in the way she goes about it.

She confides in her colleague that she feels unease at the intrusiveness of their new manager's style and at the brusqueness of his manner. She finds that her colleague has similar concerns. But this apparently trusting self-disclosure is a smokescreen to lull her colleague into a false sense of security and leave her thinking that nothing material has changed in their working relationship. In reality, however, she starts to use adversarial tactics against her colleague around the office while positioning herself to her new boss as the more trustworthy and competent of the two colleagues. And this approach spells trouble for her erstwhile peer and business friend, who can have no clue what is about to happen.

The second peer's plan consists of two strands. First, she starts to reduce her colleague's influence in the office while making it sound as if she is still enjoying working with her. She tells her peer that as far as she is concerned their partnership still remains effective, and by being open about her dislike of her new manager's style, creates the impression that she is just as trusting and open as she was before he arrived. But, on the quiet, she starts to cut her colleague out of information-giving and decision-making loops, and so removes power from her around the office. Second, she starts to drop doubts about the competence of her colleague into the mind of their boss. At first she simply makes slighting remarks about her peer to him, but when he doesn't object to this tactic, she escalates her campaign by making increasingly undermining and derogatory comments about her colleague to him. And when she judges the moment right, she attacks.

She suggests to their boss that her peer isn't up to the job and that she ought to be placed in sole charge of the pharmacy. She is clever in the way she goes about it, in that she positions this suggestion as having a benefit for her boss. She tells him that it will free up more of his time to manage his profile with his own bosses. She senses that he is an ambitious character, keen to promote himself to the senior hospital managers, and she plays on his wish for advancement. But what could account for her desire to sideline her peer, remove power from her, damage her reputation in the eyes of their manager, and place herself in sole charge of the pharmacy?

Simply put: power. She experiences her new boss's style as being about his power over her, and decides that the best way to handle *him* is to take power away from her peer, retain it for herself, and create a role for herself as her new boss's sole aide. She forms the view that she is likely to be safer working this way, in a position where she can make managing his perceptions a high priority, and thereby hopes to secure some power for herself in her dealings with him. She forms the view that working in this way will ultimately be more appealing for her than working jointly with a peer for a joint boss. It is a high-risk strategy for two reasons. First, if she does gain the trust of a manager who is bound up in his own authority, she risks incurring his wrath if he decides at any point that she has failed him. Second, she risks creating an enemy in her erstwhile peer, who will presumably still be working in the dispensary, even if in a less influential role, and who could also change her modus operandi and make trouble for her duplicitous co-worker. Nonetheless, the second peer sizes up the situation and decides that these are risks worth taking. Let's take a look at the power issues behind her decision.

Her previous boss was non-hierarchical in his approach to managing his two pharmacists. He did not feel the need to handle his team members in a way that made his relationship with them about his organizational authority over them, and consequently neither of them felt uncomfortable or put-upon when dealing with him. Equally, his trusting and open style brought the best out of both of them, and neither of them felt the need to regard the other as a rival. In fact, the three of them worked well together, and commented on this fact regularly. But the new manager uses his authority differently from his predecessor, and makes it clear from the beginning that 'he is the boss.' Neither of the pharmacists responds well to his style, and they speak openly to one another of their dismay at working for an authoritarian manager. But only one of the pharmacists uses the arrival of their new manager as a reason to justify a radical change in attitude towards her colleague.

This peer starts to see her colleague as an adversary, an opponent whom she wishes to eliminate. Rather than decide that the two of them need to stick together and support one another as they find their feet with their new manager, she decides to go it alone. She determines that she will forsake her colleague and instead ally with their boss, even though he is a man she doesn't know well, doesn't like, and is quite intimidated by. Her strategy is to create an alliance with a boss whom she fears so that she can look for ways of ingratiating herself with him while also manipulating his perceptions of her, her effectiveness, and should she decide to include them in her maneuverings, her staff.

She cannot know for sure what his reaction will be to her planned attack on her colleague's credibility and competence. He may view it dimly, he may admire it, or he may fail to see it for what it is and take it at face value. She proceeds slowly, making slighting comments about her peer at first, dropping them into conversations with her boss just to see how he reacts. When he doesn't react unfavorably to her comments she continues to make them, upping the stakes bit by bit. Simultaneously, she starts to remove information and decisions from her colleague in the hope that she might start to make mistakes that she could then draw to the attention of their manager. Eventually, having laid the groundwork, she seizes her opportunity and suggests to him that she alone should run the pharmacy, and that it would be better for his career if he arranged things this way.

The appointment of the new manager changes the power dynamic in the dispensary office. The power dynamic shifts from one where, under their old manager, power was not an issue between the peers or between them and him, to one where, under their new manager, it is *the* issue between them all. This alteration in the power dynamics is the catalyst for the second peer to reveal a ruthless and duplicitous side to her character, a side that up until that point in their relationship her peer could not have known anything about.

Should her tactics prevail and the second peer be asked to run the dispensary single-handed, she may well decide to alter her behavior towards her now defeated foe and re-adopt her usual non-adversarial approach. Only time will tell. But her selective adversarial conduct will be all the more difficult for her peer to deal with, as the two of them have worked so closely with one another before the second peer's change of heart. Had their working relationship been more distant, the second peer's attack on her colleague might have represented less of a betrayal than it will likely do given their daily proximity. The first peer now has a serious decision to make, one that may go some way to defining her future with the hospital. How will she react to her colleague's selective adversarial behavior?

So far we have been examining a situation in which a colleague who has previously used non-adversarial behavior starts to use an adversarial approach in response to her perception that the power dynamics in the office have altered. What about a different situation, one in which a team manager uses adversarial tactics selectively with a colleague whom she regards as likely to pose a threat to her carefully arranged working world? Consider the following example, which is set in the finance group of a retail bank.

CASE STUDY 7: OVERSTEPPING THE MARK

The head of finance in a retail bank is known for her effective management of her team. She reports to the CEO, who is a precise, slightly antagonistic, and driven character. The head of finance manages her team tightly and meets with each of her team leaders on a weekly basis. She expects each of them to be self-starting, committed to continuous process improvement, and actively engaged in continual self-development. She expects them to use open and trusting behavior with one another at all times, and has absolutely no time for closed or uncooperative behavior, which she thinks hinders team work and reduces the quality of work done by the team as a whole. She regularly tells her team leaders that they are employed to work with one another, not against one another.

The head of finance herself generally uses open and trusting behavior. She gives a straight answer to a straight question, is informative and candid about what she does know and clear about what she doesn't know. She is not known for being either friendly or warm, but her team members appreciate the above-board and transparent way in which she handles them, and usually manage to overlook her lack of amiability and charm.

One of her team leaders, however, starts to over-step the mark. This team leader moves into the finance group from the bank's operations team, and arrives with a strong recommendation from the operations manager who employed him previously. A self-confessed perfectionist, this team leader works long hours, pays minute attention to detail, and initiates a number of effective improvements to his team's processes. However, he also starts to spend more time with his manager than anyone else among his peer group, and starts to demand more of her emotional energy.

At first, his meetings with her run only a few minutes over time. On these occasions he waits until near the end of the meeting and then brings up an issue which he says he 'just wants to run past' her. While these issues do contain some degree of importance, they often lack urgency. His boss thinks he should be using her time more carefully, and says so. Instead of taking the feedback on board, the team leader ignores it. On each of the two subsequent meetings he again raises issues late on with his manager, issues which she thinks he ought to be handling himself. These particular issues focus on matters between his team members, and she does not feel the need to involve herself in them. She tells him so, expecting that as he has now had the same feedback twice, he will see fit to take it on board and desist from raising similar issues with her in the future. He appears to take the hint, and after not extending any of his next three meetings with her, he then asks her if he might be included in upcoming deliberations over the group's budget. The head of finance regards issues to do with the budget as her province, and is not at all pleased at this, as she sees it, impertinent request. She tells him in no uncertain terms that if she catches him getting involved with the budget she will take a very dim view of it indeed. She then informs him that the meeting is over, and waits for him to leave her office.

From this point onwards her behavior towards this team member changes. It moves from being non-adversarial, open, and collaborative to being adversarial. She no longer takes the time to address issues that he brings to their weekly meetings, but only addresses the issues she has for him. She is clipped and curt with him, more demanding of him and less inclined to include him in team problem-solving and decision-making processes. She bides her time, and after one month of using this more distant, less trusting, and less supportive behavior with him, she relents. It is not natural for her to use so much adapted behavior with one member of her team, and she finds it draining to do so. She also doesn't like leaving him out in the cold even though she thinks it a necessary move if she is to signal her displeasure to him firmly and clearly. In fact it creates an internal conflict for her to use so much adversarial behavior with someone on her own management team. So, after one month of using this approach with him, she decides that he must have got the message by now, and relents. She feels reasonably sure that he will have learned from the experience and will be unlikely to overstep the mark again.

However, the team leader doesn't really do himself any favors when, three days after the head of finance softens her approach to him, he tells her that he finds her moods quite difficult to deal with and thinks she is a challenging person to work for. The head of finance becomes very still. She sits upright in her chair and waits for a few seconds. Then she tells him in a crisp tone that she does not welcome his intrusive and personal comments. From that moment onwards the head of finance regards this team member with increasing suspicion, seeing him as someone who thinks too highly of himself, doesn't respect her position or her boundaries, and doesn't know how to handle himself politically. She systematically reduces his influence around the office, removes responsibility from him, and decreases his workload until, three weeks after his ill-judged comments, she suggests to him that his talents would be better employed in the operations team and asks him to return there.

Overstepping the Mark: Analyzing the Dynamics

Let's revisit this situation and analyze the dynamics in it. We will start by exploring the motivation and character of the head of finance and the new team leader in some detail. Then we will examine what intrapersonal factors in each of them initially causes the head of finance to use adversarial behavior towards her newest team leader before exploring how, after a period of time in which she returns to her more usual non-adversarial demeanor, their working relationship completely breaks down.

In this example, a retail bank's head of finance works hard to extend trust and support to her team members even though she is not naturally skilled with people. She handles her role as effectively as she can, using behavior that is both open and straightforward to deal with, even though she is not that comfortable working closely with people. She demands similar behavior from her team leaders and team members. With her team leaders she is particularly exacting. She expects them to work hard for their employer, continually develop their offer to the bank, and manage their teams with dedication. Moreover, she expects each of them to demonstrate cooperative and collaborative behavior at all times, conduct which she role models in her dealings with them despite the fact that it does not come easily to her to do so. She expects her team leaders to be self-sufficient, independent, and autonomous, and when they are, things work out well.

The head of finance has made a significant emotional investment in the boundaries she places around her time and her responsibilities. She takes her position and its duties very seriously. She makes it a priority to role model behavior that is open and collaborative, even though this means overriding her natural instincts, which are to be risk-averse and cautious around people. But there are limits to what she can give, and even though she works hard to create and sustain an effective, cooperative team, it is difficult for her to work closely with people all day, every day. It takes commitment and effort for her to carry off this aspect of her role, and she can only give what she is able to give. So, to counter-balance being 'out on a limb' in this way, she holds certain duties very dear and regards them as her province only. These duties include managing the budget, and she makes sure that she is the only person with access to these figures. Her emotional attachment to managing the budget single-handedly is strong. Working with numbers creates some degree of certainty and safety for her in the busy community in which she works, and it is her way of compensating for the internal stress she experiences by being professionally tightly knit to her team members.

When a new team leader joins her group, one highly recommended by the previous operations manager for whom he worked, the early signs are positive. He is conscientious, hard working, and has good ideas. However, from the moment he starts to ask her for more than she wants to give, the new team leader and his boss are on a collision course.

Like his boss, the new team leader is a complicated character. At once a perfectionist and someone with a high need for approval from his manager, the new team leader initially seems an ideal addition to the finance team. However, things start to change quite quickly when he begins to demand more time and attention from his boss than she is equipped to provide him with. The issues he chooses to raise with her at the end of their weekly update meetings are never totally frivolous, but nonetheless they do not seem to the head of finance to be matters that he ought to be putting to her. She tells him so in straightforward and clear terms. It doesn't occur to her that he will simply be unable to hear her. It doesn't occur to her that the issues he raises are actually not that pressing in and of themselves, but that it is his *underlying need for attention and approval* that is.

In raising these issues with his boss the team leader is actually trying to meet his own internally generated need for her approval, although he approaches things so badly that his manager could be forgiven for not realizing it. His request to be involved in the upcoming budget deliberations is a clumsy attempt to gain admittance to an inner area of the life of the team, an area that the head of finance regards as private and sacrosanct and to which she has not invited him. In the mind of the foolish team leader, being involved in this particular task would signal his boss's approval of him, and he goes ahead with his request without thinking it through from any perspective but his own. He badly misjudges the situation, and is subject to one month's adversarial conduct from his boss as a result of, as his boss sees it, violating one of her cherished workplace boundaries.

However, she does not like behaving in this way, and after four weeks, a long time to her, she relents. She is certain that he must have got the message by now, and that the discomfort of the past month will have been worth it. But it soon becomes clear that he hasn't got the message at all. He oversteps the mark again, and gives her feedback on how difficult he finds it working for a moody boss. Outwardly she is professional as she tells him crisply that she does not welcome his personal and intrusive feedback. But inwardly she snaps. She is furious that he has dared to address her in such terms, and she starts a campaign aimed at removing him from her team. She sees him as a loose cannon, someone who does not respect her or her position, and someone with no political common sense at all. She regards his unhelpful degree of naivety and immaturity as irredeemable blemishes on his character, and decides to engineer a situation in which she ousts him from her group. Her renewed adversarial behavior towards him includes reducing his influence around the office and taking tasks away from him, a process which continues until she judges the moment right to suggest to him that he would be better off returning to the operations team. This suggestion marks the complete breakdown of their working relationship, and even the thick-skinned team leader can have no doubt that his time is up.

In the above example, it is the degree of pressure that the naïve and emotionally unaware team leader places upon his boss which results in him experiencing her selective adversarial nature. He places her in a position that her fragile boundaries and natural reserve cannot tolerate, and he creates so much tension in their working relationship that she behaves in an adversarial manner towards him. It is the head of finance's *perception* that she needs to behave in such a radically altered way that is the key to understanding her conduct. She feels the need to turn on her team member because she regards him as being guilty of placing intolerable pressure on her, albeit unconsciously. So someone who is otherwise conscientious and principled becomes ruthless, and after he errs a second time, she sets about eliminating her opponent from her team.

BOUNDARY CONFLICTS: A KEY UNDERLYING ISSUE

Very often, although not always, the incident that is causal to a largely non-adversarial colleague starting to use adversarial behavior involves a perceived boundary conflict. In other words, the colleague who switches from non-adversarial to adversarial behavior does so because they consider that you, whether or not you agree with them, have stepped over the mark and into territory that they regard as personal or sacrosanct, and having stepped over that line you cannot now step back. An apology won't do it. Promises not to do it again probably won't do it either, although you can try. By stepping over the line once, even unintentionally, you have signaled a new phase in your relationship with your colleague, and your actions have changed the nature of the dynamic between the two of you.

You will now have to deal with your colleague's adversarial persona, and with the different sets of behaviors and altered attitudes that accompany this modus operandi. All of this may be quite radically different from the approach this colleague took with you before you made an error of judgment, albeit a possibly unintentional one. You will not be able to 'change them back again' into their non-adversarial self. Only they can do that when and if they judge the time is right, and in some situations, such as those illustrated at the conclusion of the second example, they may not want to 'switch back' at all. For those of you who find yourself in this position, your job becomes one of handling the adversarial behaviors you are faced with as effectively as possible, and the rest of this book will point you in the right direction.

CASE STUDY 8: ADDRESSING THE ISSUES

However, as well as handling the adversarial behavior your erstwhile non-adversarial colleague is now using, you can also try and address the perceived boundary violation if you want to. Let's suppose that the team leader in the above example decides, at the conclusion of the period of time in which he is left out in the cold, to address the issues he has created in his relationship with his boss, instead of telling her that he finds her moody and challenging to work for. There are a number of ways in which he could approach this conversation. Let's examine three of them.

- The team leader waits for his next weekly update meeting and starts the meeting by telling his boss that he thinks she has overreacted to something, and that it might be useful to talk it all through.

■ The team leader waits for his next weekly update meeting, and at the end of the meeting, says that he knows he has got something wrong with her and assures her that it won't happen again.

■ The team leader responds to the thaw in his manager's approach to him by booking a ten-minute slot in her diary. He starts the meeting by saying that he recognizes he has overstepped the mark, and wants to talk through the issues with her. He invites her to give her perspective on what has happened between them, and listens respectfully to what she has to say.

Addressing the Issues: Analyzing the Dynamics

Let's revisit this situation to analyze the dynamics in it. In this example a team leader is subject to selective adversarial behavior by his manager, who is otherwise not inclined to use an adversarial approach with her team members. After one month she relents and starts to handle the team leader in a non-adversarial manner once more, and he decides to broach the subject of their recent dealings with one another in order to clear the air. Let's see how he gets on:

■ In the first instance, the team leader handles himself and his manager poorly. At the first weekly update meeting following the softening of his manager's attitude towards him, he begins the discussion by saying that she might have overreacted to something he has done. Although he then immediately suggests that the two of them might profitably spend some time talking through what has happened, he has already shot himself in the foot. His manager will hear his poor choice of opening words as a criticism of her judgment rather than a clumsy invitation to resolve the issues between them. His timing is off too. As an opening gambit at a first meeting with his now non-adversarial boss, this approach is simply self-defeating. The head of finance may well decide that her team leader lacks both the interpersonal acumen and the intrapersonal awareness to re-establish credibility with her.

■ In the second instance, the team leader again misses the mark, although perhaps less obviously so. He tells his boss that he recognizes that he has done something to upset her, but he doesn't then go on to say what. Instead he tells her that 'it' won't happen again. On the surface this could appear to be a useful apology, but a closer look reveals that it actually isn't that effective. To his boss this inexact and imprecise acceptance of wrongdoing won't provide her with a level of reassurance to which she will respond favorably. She needs to hear him say that he acknowledges that he must handle the boundaries around his contact with her differently, and that he respects that he is welcome to discuss some issues with her but not others. Anything less than this clear and unambiguous statement of the way in which he intends to amend his conduct with her could leave the head of finance feeling unimpressed. In the absence of such clarity, she might conclude that while the team leader does realize that he has erred, he doesn't actually know in what way he has got it wrong, even though he wants to smooth things over. She may well be left thinking that, if he doesn't know what he has done wrong, he could do it again or do something worse, and she may simply not be satisfied with this state of affairs.

■ In the third instance, the team leader does a good job of handling his boss. By arranging a meeting with her specifically at which to discuss the issues between them, he sends her the clear message that he takes what has happened between them seriously and wants to make amends. He makes a good start to the meeting by taking responsibility for having stepped over the line and by inviting his boss to give him her perspective on the issues. This overture will go down well with the head of finance, who will hear it as a genuine attempt to learn from what has happened and make amends for any wrong-doing. Having made such a good start it is vital that the team leader capitalizes on it and responds well to what she says to him. He must not interrupt her, contradict her, avoid addressing what she says to him, or put the ball back into her court. Instead, he needs to listen respectfully to her point of view, and acknowledge that he has heard it. This combination of active listening and a willingness to take responsibility for the impact of his actions on her will encourage his boss to form the view that he is genuinely trying to learn from his mistakes and make good what has gone wrong between them. Because she is basically a principled woman who does not use adversarial tactics lightly, as long as he avoids repeating his misdemeanor, he stands a good chance of re-establishing credibility with her.

ADDRESSING THE ISSUES: A WORD OF WARNING

We have been examining ways of addressing the issues between you should you find yourself subject to selective adversarial behavior from a previously non-adversarial co-worker. In the third instance described above the team leader wisely waits until his manager reverts back to a non-adversarial stance before arranging to have an open and collaborative problem-solving conversation with her. In doing so, he takes the calculated risk that she will respond favorably to the right approach handled in the right way.

But taking this tack is advisable only when you are dealing with a selective adversarial colleague who has reverted back into non-adversarial mode, and whom you have already experienced handling their working relationship with you along trusting and supportive lines. It is not advisable to take this approach when you are dealing with a colleague who is only and always in adversarial mode, or one who is intermittently but regularly adversarial. In this case, should you attempt to discuss the issues between you in the open and collaborative manner described above, you may well find that all you have succeeded in doing is handing more power over to your oppositional-minded co-worker. Instead, you need to select and use tactics specifically tailored to the challenge of handling a colleague who only and always uses adversarial behavior. Chapters 5–7 of this book will point you in the right direction.

Each of these chapters focuses on the challenges of working with, in chapter order, adversarial peers, adversarial team members, and adversarial managers. In each of these chapters the assumption made is that the colleague with whom you are dealing is continually adversarial in mindset, rather than being selectively so as in this chapter. Each chapter explores the specific dynamics involved in the relationship with your adversarial colleague, and highlights more and less effective ways of handling them.

YOUR ADVERSARIAL COLLEAGUES

You may now like to take a moment to apply the material from this chapter to your own working life. You can jot down your answers to the following questions in the space below:

■ Identify a situation in which a colleague with whom you had worked well previously started to use selective adversarial behavior with you. In what ways did their behavior change, and how did you handle it at the time?

■ Looking back on it now, what factors do you think resulted in your colleague adopting an adversarial behavior? And what factors caused them to switch back to using non-adversarial behavior?

■ Identify a situation in which you used selective adversarial behavior in your dealings with a colleague whom you had not previously handled in this way. What happened to cause you to switch approach? What impact did using these methods have on your long-term working relationship with this colleague?

■ If you were faced with the same set of circumstances in future, what if anything would you do differently, and why?

SUMMARY AND NEXT CHAPTER

This chapter has focused on the issues involved in working with colleagues who employ selective adversarial behavior, as opposed to those who only and always employ adversarial tactics. The chapter has suggested that one of the antecedent factors in an otherwise non-adversarial colleague switching into a selectively adversarial mindset is a perceived shift in the power dynamics in the workplace. It has also suggested that perceived boundary violations could result in a largely non-adversarial colleague starting to use selective adversarial methods. The chapter has highlighted the fact that should you be subject to selective adversarial behavior you will not be able to 'switch your colleague back' into non-adversarial mode. Only they can make this decision for themselves when and if they want to. Your role, should you find yourself working alongside a selectively adversarial colleague, is to handle their adversarial behavior as best you can for as long as it continues, and to wait until they relent before trying to address the issues between you, if you want to. The chapter concluded by identifying a number of more and less effective ways of opening up a collaborative problem-solving conversation with a selectively adversarial colleague who has reverted to non-adversarial mode, and it also provided you with an opportunity to apply the material to your own working life.

The next chapter focuses on the skills and strategies you need to employ should you find yourself working with adversarial peers, colleagues with whom you need to work to get things done but over whom you have no seniority or authority. The chapter will highlight how to work with an adversarial peer so that, by and large, you can get done the things you need to get done while making sure that you limit the options your peer has for acting against you.

CHAPTER 5

Working with Adversarial Peers

Minimizing the Risk of Working without Authority and with Little Influence

This chapter will examine the dynamics of working with adversarial peers. It will highlight how to get things done with a peer who is inimical towards you but with whom you have to work anyway. The chapter will explore the ins and outs of working in a situation in which, by the very nature of the relationship, you have no authority over your peer and cannot direct them to follow your instructions, and in which you may feel that you have little influence with them either. Nonetheless you have to find ways of working effectively with your adversarial peer so that, between you, you can get done the things you need to get done, accepting that there will inevitably be some risk involved in trying to do so. This chapter will identify specific ways of reducing that risk, as well as highlight the pitfalls you may fall into should you fail to handle the situation effectively.

The chapter will examine a variety of circumstances involving working with an adversarial peer. It will begin by focusing on how to respond to an adversarial peer who wants to involve you in their work, before exploring how to involve an adversarial peer in your own work, while minimizing the risks associated with doing so in both cases. It will then move on to discuss how to influence an adversarial peer towards adopting a course of action you want them to take, but which they instinctively want to oppose. Finally, it will highlight how to react when a number of adversarial peers simultaneously decide to turn on you just to see what reaction they can get and how far they can push you. The chapter will highlight principles for handling each of these sets of circumstances effectively, illustrate these principles using realistic examples, and take a look at your own experiences of working with adversarial peers.

HANDLING AN ADVERSARIAL PEER

Working with an adversarial peer can feel like a risky thing to do. You cannot count on them to apply themselves to your joint work in a straightforward and unambiguous fashion. You cannot leave them to their own devices for fear that they might not handle things in ways you feel comfortable with, or in some cases for fear that they might not handle them at all. However, neither can you hover over them and watch what they are up to all the time. You have no authority over a peer, and in cases where you are working with a strongly adversarial colleague, may feel as if you have little influence with them either. But nonetheless you have to find ways of working with your peer so that the work gets done, you don't feel unduly vulnerable during the process of getting it done, and you keep the possibility of your peer acting against you to an acceptable level. The challenge you face is how to do this effectively and safely when your peer's untrustworthy streak might result in them trying to take advantage of any latitude you give them.

In any situation involving an adversarial peer, and no matter what the specific dynamics of the scenario might be, it would simply be unwise to hand over control of a piece of work to them for fear that they will:

- Fail to meet the deadline for completing it.
- Apply themselves to the work half-heartedly.
- Pass the work on to someone else and wash their hands of it.
- Return the work to you unfinished.
- Take advantage of the situation in some other way so that they act against you, your reputation, or your best interests.

Rather than relinquish control of the work you need to act judiciously, soliciting the input of your peer under conditions that you determine, and which you monitor closely. It is in the nature of an adversarial peer to take advantage of opportunities to act against you should they perceive them to exist. So, if you are going to work with an adversarial peer, you need to limit their options for misbehaving. The key question you need to apply yourself to is:

- How do you arrange the boundaries of the relationship so that, when you work with your peer on specific tasks, you retain control over the process of the work and over the factors that you consider being central to you achieving your goals and protecting your interests?

Consider the following example, which is set in a university geology department.

CASE STUDY 9: FISHY BUSINESS

A university geology department prints a lighthearted yearly magazine which it then distributes to its staff and students each Christmas. Members of staff volunteer to write articles for the magazine, contributing pieces on issues of interest to the department's students and their faculty colleagues. The editorship of the magazine rotates each year among the senior faculty members, and most editors begin planning for that year's publication in early September.

In late November one of faculty staff decides that she would like to write an article for the magazine, and approaches the editor. The editor is surprised that this particular faculty member wants to become involved in writing for the magazine. He regards her as an adversarial member of staff, someone capable of sly and underhand behavior when minded to do so. Nevertheless, he is short of articles for the publication, and agrees that the piece she suggests does sound interesting. He gives her the go-ahead to write it.

The faculty staff member is delighted, and approaches one of her colleagues for an interview. The colleague whose input she solicits is a researcher who also works in the geology department. He is a peer of hers, a quieter character than her, someone steadfast and talented at his job. The faculty member tells her peer that she would like to write an article for the magazine, and that she has already secured the interest of the editor for a piece involving him. She tells him that she would like to write about both him and the book that he has recently self-published. She tells him that she has heard good feedback on his book, which is about Pacific Island fishing communities. She informs him that the book will make an interesting angle for her article, which will partly be a review of the work and partly a piece about its author.

The researcher is pleased to be approached for the interview, and he accepts the invitation to participate. He knows of his peer more by reputation than through experience, and is aware of her adversarial character. Nonetheless, this will be the first interview he gives about his recently published book, and he thinks that the publicity, even though it will be in-house rather than to the academic community at large, will be useful. The interview is arranged for the following day, and the researcher books a meeting room for the occasion. Thirty minutes before the meeting is due to start, he receives a telephone call from his colleague telling him that she is working at home that day. She requests that they hold the interview over the telephone, and he agrees. The interview only takes ten minutes and on its completion, despite not having raised the issue beforehand, the researcher asks how the recording of the interview will be used.

He is surprised to hear his colleague say that she hasn't recorded the interview but has taken notes in shorthand instead. She then says that although she can write shorthand she cannot decode it. The researcher thinks this is highly unlikely, and becomes immediately suspicious. He thinks his colleague is being disingenuous, and says that he would like to see the article before it is published. The faculty member declines his request. She says that if she allowed him access to the article before it was published, she would have to make that exception for everyone.

The researcher is bemused by this confused series of messages. In the pause that follows her last statement the faculty member ends the call smartly, leaving the researcher feeling distinctly uncomfortable. He doesn't know what to do next. While he would like to see what the faculty member writes before it is published, he doesn't think he will have much success pursuing the point. After some thought, he reluctantly decides that there isn't much he can do except wait for the magazine to be circulated. When the magazine is published one month later, it does contain a piece by the faculty member. As promised, she includes a review of the researcher's book alongside an article about him and his work. Sadly, the review of the researcher's book is scathing and the article includes a series of apparent quotations from him which he does not recognize, none of which paint him in a light he likes.

Furious that his trust as been betrayed by a colleague who can have no good reason for acting against him, he calls the senior colleague who has edited this edition of the magazine to complain about her conduct. The editor's assistant says he is busy, so the researcher asks to be put through to his voicemail, on which he leaves a message. He informs the editor that the latest edition of the magazine, one he edited, contains an unwarranted and mischievous article about him including quotations purporting to come from him, but which he does not recognize. He says that it also includes an error-strewn and factually inaccurate review of his recently published book. He tells the editor's voicemail that he acted in good faith in giving the faculty member concerned input for her article, and thinks she has behaved poorly towards him.

When the editor replies it is on email and ten days later. He says that he has spoken to the faculty member involved, and that as the article and book review reflect her personal views on the subjects she has written about, there is nothing he is prepared to do about the situation. By this time the researcher has had to field a number of comments from his peer group and his students, each of which is either a joke at his expense or a genuine enquiry about how such a rude piece of writing could have been printed about him in the faculty magazine.

Fishy Business: Analyzing the Dynamics

Let's revisit this situation to analyze the dynamics in it. We will explore the motivation of the faculty member, and highlight how, had the researcher and newly published author handled the boundaries around his involvement with her differently and more proactively, he might not have had his fingers so badly burned.

In this example a geology faculty member calls one of her peers to ask for his input to an article she wants to write on him and his self-published book. The peer knows of this faculty member from a distance and is aware of her adversarial reputation. However he is pleased, even flattered, at her interest in his work and his book and, caught off-guard by an enquiry he welcomes, he accepts the invitation of an interview for her article. While it wouldn't be true to say that he trusts her, it is true to say that he is open to her and doesn't actively mistrust her. And herein lies the problem. He totally misunderstands her approach. It does not cross his mind that her innocent-sounding invitation could be the prelude to a betrayal of his trust. He does not realize that the faculty member is setting him up for a fall, and that whatever he says in the interview and no matter how interesting, accurate, or knowledgeable he proves to be on his subject matter, she will write a scathing review of his book and distribute it to the entire staff and student population of the faculty via the yearly magazine. He doesn't even suspect these things, and sadly leaves himself wide open to an unprovoked attack on his reputation and standing in the department. He approaches the project in a naïve way, treating his colleague with professional courtesy. He then provides her with a degree of latitude which she has not earned, and which leaves him vulnerable to her oppositional streak. That said, he is dealing with a particularly unpleasant colleague, one who uses her position as a contributor to the Christmas magazine to attack him for no good reason at all. Let's take a look at what could motivate her to act in this way.

The faculty member is bored. She is on the look out for something interesting to do, and decides to contribute to the Christmas magazine. When she gets the green light to write the piece she has in mind, she seizes the opportunity to indulge her adversarial instincts and attack her unsuspecting research colleague. She acts this way partly because she enjoys the power this course of action gives her, and partly because she wants to burst the bubble of a researcher who sounds pleased to be approached when she first speaks to him. She has a malicious side to her character, and this side of her wants to destroy his enjoyment at being the subject of an article. This is a mean thing to do, and one for which she can have no real justification. It probably doesn't occur to her to handle things this way before she speaks to the researcher. But on hearing his voice and listening to his evident pleasure at being approached, she makes up her mind. She decides it will be fun to use the interview and article to have a go at him in public through the medium of the magazine.

While he can be forgiven for not expecting her to be as underhand as she is, the researcher's disengaged and naïve approach to the project does him no favors. He gives the faculty member additional room for maneuver from the off. He sets no boundaries around his involvement with her. He does nothing to protect himself while dealing with someone whose character is not proven to him and who he knows has a suspect reputation. He agrees to the interview without checking in advance how the faculty member will use the material he gives her. He doesn't ask her why she wants to write for the magazine, or what she has written for it before. Nor does he ask her what kind of piece she wants to write, or what access he can have to the unpublished article before it goes to print. Instead, he assumes goodwill on her part. He assumes that she will handle the assignment in as good-natured a way as he would do had their roles been reversed. This is a big assumption to make on his part, and one for which there is no evidence. He doesn't even question her when 30 minutes before their planned meeting, the faculty member calls him and requests a telephone interview instead of a face-to-face interview. He doesn't hear the alarm bell that should have been ringing in his head at this point, and blithely agrees to the changed method of interview. And it all backfires on him badly towards the end of the telephone interview, when the adversarial faculty member gives the game away.

She is so enamored of her own trickery and duplicity that she actually tells the researcher that she can write shorthand but cannot decode it, something that obviously cannot be true. If she can write it then she *can* decode it. He is quite rightly concerned at what is clear dishonesty, and for the first time, worries that she might not be a good person to deal with. But by now he has given the interview and it is too late. He tries to redeem the situation by asking to see the piece before it is published. But she refuses his request with woolly words about not wanting to let him see the unpublished article as that would mean she would have to let everyone else do so too, a statement which is a further example of her unclear use of words and her dishonest and insincere nature.

The researcher is undone. There is nothing he can do to prevent the faculty member from submitting her article for publication, and he has nothing concrete to go on except his own fears about what she might write. He decides against ringing the editor and sharing his concerns with him, as without any evidence, he thinks he will sound paranoid. Sadly though, his fears prove justified. He reads the article upon publication and is horrified to discover that the faculty member has written a damning piece about his book and misquoted him in her article. His peer group and students talk to him about the article and he feels embarrassed. To add insult to injury the researcher then has to endure the fact that the magazine editor backs up the faculty member when he subsequently complains about her conduct.

So what could the researcher have done differently at the start of his involvement with the faculty member to protect him from her adversarial nature?

First, he needs to demonstrate much more personal resolve in his dealings with the faculty member, and be more actively engaged in the process of working with her from the first moment they speak. He does know of her adversarial reputation, but he foolishly ignores what he knows. He puts to one side his concerns about her conduct as a colleague, and makes a series of naïve assumptions about her intentions regarding the interview. He ascribes benign motives to her *because he wants to see her as good,* and does so without having any evidence to support this view. Instead of simply deciding that she will represent him well in her article, he needs to take steps to find out whether or not she will do so. There are a number of ways in which he could have done this. He could have insisted that the two of them meet for a face-to-face interview rather than carry out the hastily rescheduled interview over the telephone. The dual benefits of handling things this way are that it gives him the chance to size up his colleague's character face-to-face as well as giving him the option of taping or videoing the interview itself. This approach will provide him with a much-needed record of what he says and what he does not say, and give him concrete grounds for complaining to the editor and faculty member should he subsequently need to.

Alternatively, if the faculty member refuses to meet him for a face-to-face interview, and he still wants to go ahead with the interview that day, the researcher needs to insist that the interview takes the form of a series of written questions and replies. The faculty member could pose as many questions as she likes to him on email, and he could then provide her with written answers to each of them in a secure .pdf. The benefit of this approach is that the researcher will have a written record of his replies to her questions and will be able to prove what he has and what he has not said should he subsequently need to do so.

Either way, the researcher needs to start his dealings with the faculty member in a different place. The first time they speak he needs to ask her some pithy questions, questions designed to give him an opportunity to size up her character and form a view about her intentions for the article. He could ask her, 'What is your interest in Pacific Island fishing communities?' and listen to her answer. He could ask her, 'What is the angle you are choosing for your article?' and listen to her answer. He could ask her: 'What would make this article really enjoyable to write from your point of view?' or 'What leads you to want to write about me?' and listen to her answers. The trick is in how he interprets her responses. If she says, for instance, that she is a fisherwoman herself, is looking to publicize the plight of small fishing communities, and thinks that, as he has recently written a book, it would be a good time to draw attention to the issues, then he can feel reasonably safe that she is a well-intentioned faculty member. Or if she says that she has always wanted to visit the Pacific Islands but hasn't yet had a chance to do so, and thought his book would enable her to learn about them prior to visiting, he might again think he is on reasonably firm ground. But, if she makes ambivalent and vague responses that don't clarify the nature of her interest in his book, he ought to be on alert from that moment onwards. What clues does he need to listen out for?

The faculty member's tone and choice of words are all-important. She might use a manner and employ phraseology that is neither open nor transparent, but that is indirect and oblique. She might say that she wants to write a piece about a colleague and what he is doing, but not say anything specific about why she has selected him. She might say that she needs a theme to write about, but not clarify what that theme is or how it relates to him. Or she might say that she wants to draw attention to the people who work in the faculty, again without adding anything exact to clarify what he has to do with these aims. On the surface these answers appear to be reasonable enough responses. But a closer look reveals that they are not. They are answers that are designed to sound OK and to lull an unsuspecting listener into a false sense of security, but they are actually words that create a smokescreen behind which she can do as she pleases. They are signals that she is not that clear herself what she is going to write about, and is on the lookout for, as she sees it, an interesting angle. And given her adversarial nature, that angle might spell trouble for the researcher.

Only someone listening really hard would hear the purposeful ambiguity in these responses. Had the faculty member given a reply along any of these lines to questions designed to probe her character and her intentions for her article, the researcher would need to consider pulling out of the interview, no matter how disappointed he may be at taking this course of action. He would need to seriously consider whether, given her ambivalent and vague responses, he wants to take the risk of working with this faculty member, and whether it might not be wiser to let her look elsewhere for material for her article. The alternative is that he places his reputation in the hands of an unscrupulous peer who writes a scurrilous piece about him and distributes it to the entire faculty staff and students for no reason other than that she enjoys doing so.

Lastly, the researcher needs to make a much better fist of complaining to the editor. Again, he assumes that the editor will be as scandalized on receiving his complaint as he is on reading the piece about him. But the editor is not upset at all. In fact he can't really be bothered with his research colleague's dismay at being written about unkindly, and ignores his voice message for ten days. His reply, to the effect that his faculty members are allowed to give a personal opinion in the magazine, sends the clear message to the researcher that he can count on receiving no help from the editor, and from that moment onwards, the researcher knows that he will be powerless to right a wrong. He would have been better placed to prove his case had he retained a copy of the interview either on video, voice tape, or email, so that he could provide a comparison of what he *did* say with what was printed and attributed to him. Without such evidence, he is on a sticky wicket even though right is on his side. With such evidence, he would be better placed to insist on a retraction or an apology for being misquoted, although with such an irresponsible editor it might still be difficult for him to attain either.

MANAGING THE BOUNDARIES

We have been examining a situation in which one peer is approached by another peer with an invitation to participate in what on the surface looks like a mutually beneficial project. Only it turns out to be a nightmare for the non-adversarial peer when his adversarial colleague uses the situation to make trouble for him. Let's take a look at the key lessons from the example.

A key tool in managing an adversarial peer is your personal resolve to place effective boundaries around your peer's involvement with you and your work, and your subsequent willingness to enforce those boundaries by taking control of the situation. Deciding where to place the boundary with any peer will depend on your reading of their trustworthiness in regards to the work you are doing together. You may decide that an adversarial peer can be trusted with some aspects of the work but not with others. By setting an effective boundary around your adversarial peer's involvement on a project, you are making a clear statement to them about how much trust you are prepared to extend to them, and under what circumstances you will withdraw that trust and alter the boundary between them and the work.

It may take some hard thinking on your part to identify which boundaries to handle in what way, and therefore how much trust to extend to an adversarial peer over which issues. You probably won't be used to thinking things through in this conscious way when working with non-adversarial peers, colleagues who you don't think are likely to mishandle opportunities to work with you. But it will be worth it to make special arrangements when working with an adversarial peer so that you can limit their options for taking advantage of any room to maneuver you give them during the period in which you work together. In practice this means making decisions about:

- What information you give your peer access to.
- Which tasks you ask your peer to handle.
- Which meetings you include them in.
- What scope you give them to act independently of you on the project.
- Which decisions you involve them in.
- Which problem-solving processes you ask them to input to.
- What responsibilities you assign to them.

Being able to manage the boundaries around your work to protect you from the oppositional streak in an adversarial peer is essential.

It is essential when you decide to work with an adversarial peer for the first time, as in the case study above, or when you have to work with an adversarial peer on a consistent basis. The trick is in deciding where to place the boundaries. You need to give it some thought and decide how to arrange things so that you retain control over the factors that you think are critical to your success, while still providing sufficient latitude so that your colleague can contribute to the work.

FINDING SUITABLE BOUNDARIES: THREE SHORT EXAMPLES

So how do you decide where to place the boundary? Consider the following three short examples.

- Two peers in a training company agree to work together to produce and market a new training package for internal coaches. One of the peers regards the other as having adversarial traits. These traits result in him taking on work which he doesn't complete in a timely manner and subsequently blaming his failure to deliver on his co-workers instead of taking responsibility for it himself. The first peer determines to manage his colleague quite closely so that he can get his input to the project without finding that his reputation is sullied by his colleague's scapegoating tactic. After every meeting between the two of them about the project, the first peer produces extensive minutes and sends them to his colleague and to both of their bosses. These minutes detail what tasks each of them has agreed to complete and by when. On the first instance that his adversarial peer fails to deliver on time, this peer confronts him. He tells him that he had not received any notification from him that he would be missing a key deadline, and asks what he expects to happen next. His colleague equivocates. He is unprepared for a confrontation and is slightly thrown. Then he says that the work is 'in hand' and will be 'completed shortly.' The non-adversarial peer is not satisfied with this reply. He hears it as dissembling rather than truthful reassurance, and decides he is being fobbed off. Rather than have to face continual delays and frustrations as he waits for his colleague to complete his side of the work, he resolves then and there to cut his peer out of the project and continue the work alone. The non-adversarial peer tells his adversarial colleague firmly but clearly that he will be handling the project unilaterally from that point onwards.

He then says that if his peer objects to this course of action he will be quite willing to have the conversation he needs to have in a four-way meeting with his own boss, his colleague's boss, and his colleague. The adversarial peer sneers at him and calls him a 'boy scout who is getting hot under the collar.' He hopes that by being personally offensive he can unsettle his colleague and take back the advantage. But he misjudges the resolve of his peer who, rather than rise to the bait, merely reiterates his decision that he will complete the project alone and does so in the same steady, firm tone. This peer then leaves the room and immediately informs both managers by email that he is assuming sole responsibility for running the project from that point onwards, and that he is willing to assume personal accountability for its outcome. He copies this email to his adversarial colleague. To his mind his choice is clear: work harder and assume sole responsibility for the project or risk a hit to his reputation because he is working with an unreliable and ambivalent co-worker whom he does not trust. He prefers the former choice even though it will probably involve him in a series of uncomfortable conversations with his managers and peer, and a series of long days at work.

■ Two investment bankers are asked by their joint boss to work together on a high-profile project. One of the two is dismayed at the choice of this particular peer as his co-worker for the work. While he is quite prepared to handle himself robustly and confrontationally at work, he doesn't regard himself as an evasive or tricky co-worker to have. His past experience of this colleague is that he is both of these things, being an adversarial and a duplicitous character. Rather than take the reputational risk of saying 'no' to his boss by turning down a high-profile project, he agrees to work with the adversarial colleague provided that it is he who reports to his boss about the progress of the project on a day-to-day basis. He sells this way of working to his boss by telling that he will be much more assiduous in updating him than his colleague, and will be more effective at giving him a heads-up should anything happen on the project that he thinks his boss would like to know about. His boss agrees. The non-adversarial peer then sets up a meeting with his oppositional colleague. He starts the meeting on the front foot, bringing up a contentious issue straight away to see how his colleague will react, and to see what he can learn about his current state of mind. He mentions a project to which they both contributed the previous year, a project that did not go well. While some of the responsibility for the failure of the project lay with the non-adversarial peer, a lot more lay with the adversarial peer. At the time, this peer refused to own his misjudgments, preferring to generate a series of explanations that lessened his culpability and justified the poor outcome of the project. On being reminded of this episode at the start of this meeting, the adversarial peer smiles knowingly but doesn't say anything. His colleague ignores this reaction, and tells him that the parameters of the current project are similar to those of the previous project. He says that, mindful of how things went last time, he will handle himself differently should he find the present project going off course. He says that he will be reporting to their joint boss daily on the progress of the project, and expects that he will have positive outcomes to report day by day. Then he looks his colleague in the eye and lets a silence fall. After several seconds he says that he is a quick learner and expects similar standards from those he works with. The adversarial peer doesn't say anything and outwardly appears unmoved. However, inwardly he realizes that his peer will be a different proposition from the last time they worked together, and will likely be watching him like a hawk. He forms the view that his peer may well be prepared to act if he deems it necessary. Although at this stage he doesn't know quite what form those actions might take, he thinks that they would likely cause discomfort for him. It is now the adversarial peer who has a choice to make: work on the project and find that life becomes uncomfortable should be handle things in an untrustworthy and uncommitted way, decide to buck up his ideas and become more considered and honest in his dealings, or decline the opportunity to work on this joint task and look for other projects in the bank instead. Should he take the project, only time will tell to what extent he is able to keep his adversarial streak under check as the work progresses, but he has had a clear warning about what to expect if fails to handle himself well.

■ Two secondary school teachers are engaged on a joint research project to improve the standard of external examination results attained by the school's students. Both peers have adversarial natures. One regularly fails to act on verbal commitments she gives her colleagues, leaving the tasks undone, while the other teacher regularly says one thing but then does something quite different. Both teachers obfuscate and equivocate when their colleagues go back to them to clarify what has happened, and neither amends their ways despite having received feedback on many occasions that it would be useful if they did. On the current project, neither teacher trusts the other, and both want to handle the assignment so that their colleague has minimal opportunities to act against them. The first teacher suggests that she handle the research with the students and that her colleague handles the research with the teachers. However, her colleague prefers that they both play a role in handling the research with teachers and with students. She doesn't want to provide her colleague with any opportunity to step over the line and use the project to her own ends, even though she is not clear what form that duplicity might take. She thinks that if they both are involved in research with students and teachers she will be better placed to keep an eye on her colleague. In the end they agree to an uneasy truce whereby they conduct the research via questionnaire rather than through face-to-face interviews so that they can review the responses simultaneously and agree what recommendations to make together. This is an inefficient way to work as it involves both teachers in carrying out the same tasks at the same time, but it means that the project does proceed, albeit after some delay.

In each of the first two situations a largely non-adversarial peer is faced with the prospect of working with an adversarial peer and needs to take steps to protect their workplace interests. In each case the non-adversarial peer acts early on to lay down a clear boundary, a boundary that outlines their expectations of their peer and their conduct on the project while defining clearly the areas in which their peer's input is welcome. But, crucially, as soon as their peer appears to be sliding towards behavior that is ambivalent and unreliable, the non-adversarial peer alters that boundary to protect themselves.

In the first case, this happens after the project has begun. It results in the non-adversarial peer taking over the entire project, effectively preventing his adversarial co-worker from holding up the work, letting him down, fobbing him off, or otherwise misbehaving. In the second instance, the adversarial peer's misconduct occurs early on in the first meeting to explore how the two peers will work together. It results in a face-to-face confrontation between the two colleagues. It is the non-adversarial peer's prior agreement with their joint boss that he alone will report on the project's progress, coupled with his personal resolve to hold his errant co-worker responsible for any shenanigans, which results in his having the upper hand in this confrontation.

In both of these cases, the largely non-adversarial character finds a way to demonstrate his commitment to his stated boundaries. This is what alters the dynamic between him and his adversarial peer. Stating where he wants to place the boundary is the first step, but it is his *commitment to changing that boundary* when he suspects that their colleague is misusing the trust that is being placed with him that really counts.

However, in the third case, two adversarial colleagues cannot find a way to work together at all until they agree to carry out the same tasks simultaneously. They are both unwilling to let the other work on any aspect of the project unaided, both fearing that their colleague will act in an untrustworthy manner if given the opportunity to do so. While neither can say in what specific way they suspect that their peer might cross the line, the fact is that they both think they might. So, the only way to complete the project is via questionnaires which will be analyzed by both people in the same room at the same time. The boundary in this case is one that precludes either party from doing anything on the project without their peer being present to vet what they are doing. The mistrust between them is that great.

MANAGING THE BOUNDARIES AROUND YOUR WORK

Managing your boundaries when working with an adversarial peer is about giving specific, clear messages to your peer about:

- Areas in which you are prepared to extend trust to them.
- What input you expect from your peer within these boundaries.
- What conduct you will consider unacceptable or out of line.
- How you will react under these circumstances.

Handling the boundaries of your relationship with an adversarial peer in this way is both a self-preserving and a self-protective thing to do. With some strongly adversarial peers it is the only way to go. I have written previously about the nature of boundaries at work in Chapter 8 of *Managing Politics at Work : The Essential Toolkit for Identifying and Handling Political Behaviour in the Workplace* (2009, pp 99–107). For our purposes here, it is important to note that there is a close relationship between the extent to which you are able to manage the boundaries around your interactions with an adversarial peer, and the extent to which you are successful at protecting yourself from your peer's oppositional tactics.

Managing your boundaries effectively sends a clear message to an adversarial peer that you are:

■ One step ahead of the game.
■ Wise to their tactics.
■ Quite prepared to respond to any untoward behavior as and when it happens.

Managing your boundaries effectively prevents your adversarial peer from having the opportunity to establish an adversarial element in to their dealings with you on that project. It can be hard work to keep an eye out for infringements of your boundaries by adversarial peers when you are absorbed in your duties. However, it is essential that you do just that. An adversarial peer will likely try to push the boundary to see how committed you are to enforcing it, to see what they can get away with, and to test just how seriously you take your commitment to what you have said. Your peer may well be motivated to try again and with more serious intent if you don't act to enforce your boundaries every time they push the boundary and test your resolve.

RETAINING CONTROL OF WORK YOU ARE MANAGING

Making clear statements about where you draw the line and being prepared to back up those commitments with action enables you to retain control of the process of a project when working with an adversarial peer. And retaining control of the process of a project is a vital learned skill should you find yourself having to work regularly with a strongly adversarial peer. Learning to master this skill will result in you being better placed to:

■ Protect yourself from any unscrupulous traits in your peer.
■ Send out the message to your peer that you alone decide how much room you will give them on any piece of work, and in what specific ways you will involve them in work you are managing.
■ Avoid the anxiety you will feel should you leave yourself unprotected and vulnerable to being exploited by your peer's oppositional streak.

And it will earn you the reputation as someone who is actively involved in managing their work and the process of involving colleagues in that work. This in turn will cause those adversarial peers who look for opportunities to misbehave to think twice before taking advantage of any opportunity they perceive to act against you.

YOUR ADVERSARIAL COLLEAGUES

You may now like to take a moment to apply the material from this chapter to your own working life. You can jot down your answers to the following questions in the space below:

- Identify a situation in which you believe an adversarial peer acted against you. What was the situation and what happened in it?

- Looking back on it now, how could you have better protected yourself in that situation? What boundaries could you have altered to limit your peer's options for misbehaving?

- If you were in the same situation again, what else would you do differently to protect your interests?

So far, we have been examining situations in which you need to work with an adversarial peer and in which judicious management of your boundaries is a key self-protective tool. But what about a different situation, one in which you need to influence an oppositional peer towards adopting a new way of doing things which you favor and which they oppose? Consider the following example, which is set in a government office.

CASE STUDY 10: CUTTING THROUGH THE FOG

The technology manager of a government office decides to approach one of the directorate heads to which he and his team offer support. He regards the directorate head as an adversarial peer. She is never rude to his face. Nor does she go on the attack behind his back. But she is downright awkward to deal with, being dexterous verbally, difficult to pin down, and resistant to change. When challenged about any issue in her department by a peer, the directorate head says all the right things, makes all the right noises, but having made commitments and promises to do things differently, she simply doesn't. When subsequently confronted on her lack of progress she marshals a well-oiled toolkit of fogging, obfuscating, and justifying tactics to cloud the issue and avoid responsibility for her tardiness. She is so skilled at doing this that the colleague confronting her can leave a meeting with her thinking that he is in the wrong for enquiring about the slow progress, rather than that she is in the wrong for having failed to make anything happen. The technology manager has encountered the directorate head in full-on avoid mode before. In his previous meetings with her he has left the room tied up in knots and completely defeated. Now he wants to tackle her again, this time to encourage her to handle technology escalations in her team in a different way.

At present the directorate head calls the technology team two or three times a day to raise issues which sometimes are both urgent and important, but which more often are the product of her lack of willingness to learn the basic ins and outs of the system. Her attitude communicates itself to her team, who also call the technology office over issues that other teams would not need to refer. The technology manager has previously suggested that the directorate team would benefit from IT skills training, and has also suggested that he and his team could develop a suitable workshop specifically for them. Sadly, this idea fell on deaf ears, and his subsequent email about the subject to the directorate head went unanswered.

The technology manager decides to approach the subject again. He wants to impress upon the directorate head more forcibly that it would be in her and her team's best interests if she and they attend a one-day workshop to improve their facility with the system. He plans his argument. He wants to convey that attendance at the workshop will upgrade the directorate team's IT skills and obviate the need for them to call the technology team so often. In turn this will result in their being less dependent on his team for answers to simple issues, less frustrated at delays should his team not be able to respond immediately to their enquiries, and better able to get on with their own work independently of the IT team.

There are a number of ways in which the technology manager could handle his upcoming meeting with the directorate head. Let's examine three of them:

- The technology manager starts the meeting by outlining some statistics. He tells the directorate head that her department places between three and four times as many calls to his team as any other department. He draws breath preparatory to moving on to his renewed suggestion of IT skills training when he is thrown by an interruption from the directorate head. She tells him that they place that many calls because they are committed to providing top-quality work to the government and require effective and efficient IT support to achieve that aim. Then, without pausing for breath, she looks down at the file on her desk and with pen poised enquires what the meeting is about, because she is busy and wants to get on.
- The technology manager starts the meeting by asking the directorate head if she has considered his suggestion that she could send her team on a one-day IT skills workshop designed specifically for them by his team. The directorate head opens her mouth in astonishment, and asks him whether his team can afford to take a day off work to attend a workshop, because hers certainly can't.
- The technology manager starts the meeting by asking the directorate head what her key priorities are. She replies that her main priority is to produce first-rate work for the government. The technology head then asks her what role technology plays in her and her team achieving this aim. The directorate head replies that she could not run her department without technology. The technology manager immediately says that he has a plan to enable her to better achieve her goal of delivering first-rate work for the government, a plan that will require one day of each of her team members' time. He lets this sink in before asking her if she would be open to hearing his idea. After a short pause in which she doesn't say anything and is physically very still, the directorate manager manages to say 'yes'.

Cutting Through the Fog: Analyzing the Dynamics

Let's revisit this situation to analyze the dynamics in it and explore the motivation of the directorate head. We will then identify what difference the alternative openings used by the technology manager represent to her, and explore why she responds so differently to them.

In this example a directorate head makes inappropriate use of the technology team. Her behavior encourages her team to do the same. Between them the directorate team make three to four times as many calls per week to the technology team as any other department, and many of the calls are about such minor issues that they eat into the technology team's time ineffectively. The directorate head is adversarial in nature, but her oppositional streak is neither aggressive nor obviously inimical. It is however very real and very draining to deal with.

Her ambivalent nature shows itself in the way in which she responds to colleagues' suggestions, input, or attempts to get her to do things differently. Under these circumstances she becomes fractious, awkward, and antagonistic. She deliberately disagrees with them, rejecting their input regardless of its merits. The more her colleagues take her disagreements at face value, the stronger she becomes. She does not disagree because she has considered their input and come to a different conclusion about the issues. She disagrees because she wants to. She takes the contrary view simply because she enjoys saying 'no', enjoys thwarting her colleagues, and enjoys being in charge of a meeting. In addition, the directorate manager is very quick on her feet. She is verbally able. Her nimble verbal style results in her being able to outwit her more straight and ponderous colleagues, like the technology manager, and results in them quickly feeling defeated and drained. This is a difficult dynamic for them to deal with, and one that has previously left the technology manager tied up in knots.

The technology manager is nothing if not dogged, and despite getting nowhere in the past, he determines to have another go at persuading the directorate head to take up his offer of an IT skills workshop for her team. He arranges a meeting with her. He goes to her office ready to re-open the conversation about her sending her team members and herself on the one-day event. He hopes that this time he will manage the meeting in a way that circumvents her well-used tactics of obfuscating, fogging and avoiding the issues. Let's see how he gets on.

■ In the first instance, the technology manager starts the meeting by quoting statistics that prove how much of his team's time is being taken up by the directorate team, and that compare their use of IT with that of the other directorates. He wants to demonstrate to her that she and her team are using up his team's time inappropriately and unnecessarily, and hopes that she will volunteer, or at least work with him, to remedy this situation. His hope is a false one as she has no goodwill to offer him, and doesn't care that her team eat into his team's time. His opening is actually quite a foolish one, as it hands her the initiative. The statistics he quotes are quite accurate, but quoting them at the start of the meeting only succeeds in provoking the directorate head. She hears these facts as a litany of complaints about her and her team, and goes on the offensive. She tells the technology manager that they place that number of calls because they are committed to providing top-quality work to the government and require effective and efficient IT support to achieve that aim. This has the effect of changing the point of the conversation away from her team's inappropriate use of the technology team's time, and towards her subtle implication that the technology team might be neither effective nor efficient in supporting her team. She tops this off with an enquiry, pen poised, about the purpose of the current meeting because she is busy and wants to get on. The technology manager fails before he even starts. His opening gambit only succeeds, however unintentionally, in engaging the anger of the directorate head, who puts him down commandingly.

In the second instance, once again the technology manager starts the meeting by referring to his agenda for the meeting. He asks the directorate head if she has given any thought to his previous suggestion that the directorate staff attend a one-day workshop. In a split second the directorate head can see where this conversation is headed, and doesn't like it at all. She doesn't want, as she would see it, to have her back put up against a wall by an internal supplier, so she replies by characterizing the workshop as a day off and asks the technology manager if his staff can afford to take time off from their work, because hers are far too busy to do so. Once more, the technology manager has shot himself in the foot. Rather than open up a conversation about the benefits to the directorate of attending the workshop, his poorly handled opening to the meeting has resulted in his being roundly slapped down. It will be difficult for him to recover from such a poor start, and he might be unable to.

■   In the third instance, the technology manager plays it carefully and wisely. He does not want to risk being seen as someone coming to the directorate head's office to make demands of her or to offer her unsolicited suggestions. So he decides to craft the meeting around her key priorities and her work agenda. He starts off by *focusing on her and her agenda*, and asks her quite specifically what her key work priority is at the moment. The directorate head answers the question because it is about her, not him, and because she can see no reason not to. She tells him her key priority is to produce first-rate work for the government. The technology manager has got a straight answer to a straight question. This is a good start as far as he is concerned. Now he needs to build on this answer and make an explicit link between what the directorate head says she wants to do – serve the government well – and his own suggestion that her team attend an IT skills workshop. But he is cleverer than to come straight out with it. Instead he decides to ask her a series of questions so she can come to her own conclusions about it. So he asks her what role technology plays in her achieving her goal of serving the government excellently. He hears her say that she couldn't achieve this aim without technology. So far, so good. The technology manager now prepares to get to his key point. He tells the directorate head that he has a plan to enable her to better achieve her key priority, a plan that will require only one day of each of her team members' time. This is very smartly done, because having said that her key goal is to serve the government well, the directorate head cannot now avoid hearing a plan to help her better achieve that aim, especially one that will only take up one day of each of her team's time. In the pause that follows, the technology manager watches the directorate head's face carefully, and when he judges it right, asks her in the same neutral tone whether she is open to hearing this idea. Asking her for permission to outline his idea is another bright tactic. After a short pause in which she doesn't say anything and is physically very still, the directorate manager has to say 'yes'. She cannot say 'no' because it would imply that she is not that committed to serving the government effectively, something that would be unthinkable for someone in her position. The technology manager has created an opening for himself. Now he needs to use it carefully by outlining the benefits of attending the workshop *for the directorate, the head, her staff, and the quality of work they will subsequently be able to do for the government*. He must not make it about the benefits to him and his staff by mentioning a reduction in the number of occasions on which his staff will have to respond to directorate staff. Nor must he say that it will mean that the directorate staff will only need to escalate urgent and important items. He must keep it about her and her team and their work, by saying that they will have more time to commit to the work itself rather than waiting for IT to respond to their queries. Or that they will be better placed to use the technology capability they have to achieve better quality, higher level outputs for the government. Or that they will be less frustrated by delays caused by his team being unable to attend to them promptly. Using these arguments the technology manager has a good chance of placing the directorate head in a position where she cannot decline his offer of a workshop. He has a good chance of securing at least a pilot workshop involving two or three staff members, with the possibility of more workshops to follow should the participants report favorably on the pilot event.

CIRCUMVENTING AN OPPOSITIONAL STREAK

We have spent some time analyzing an example in which a non-adversarial peer needs to persuade an adversarial peer to do things differently even though he knows she will not initially be minded to cooperate with him. In fact, her adversarial mindset will result in her trying to oppose his suggestions on instinct even if they could benefit her in the long run. The non-adversarial peer therefore has to use a specific approach, one designed to circumvent her adversarial nature, or else he will become tied up in knots again. In order to secure her agreement to his plan he needs to adopt a carefully crafted approach, one that circumvents her oppositional streak and engages her in a discussion about her key work priorities.

Those of you who recognize the challenge of getting an adversarial peer to adopt a course of action that you favor but that they oppose on instinct may want to replicate this approach with that peer. To do so effectively you need to:

- Start the meeting by asking your peer what their key work priority is at that time.
- Listen to their answer without discussing it or commenting on it.
- Ask a second question, one that makes an explicit link between your peer's stated work priority and the course of action or agenda

item you want them to consider. This question could take the form of: 'to what extent is [the course of action/agenda item] important to you in achieving that goal?'

■ Listen the answer, again without commenting on it or discussing it.

■ Then ask your peer whether they would like to hear a suggestion you have for helping them better achieve their goal, a suggestion which will require short-term input from them and their team but which will provide long-term benefits for them.

■ Wait for them to reply 'yes' without saying anything else in the silence that follows.

■ Outline your suggestion only in terms of the benefits it will bring to your peer, their team and their work. Avoid speaking about any of the benefits to you of their adopting the course of action you want them to take, as doing so will likely engage their opposi-tional streak and they may reject your idea simply to prevent you getting what you want. Instead, outline the benefits to them of adopting the course of action you want them to adopt.

■ Ask them for their reaction to your proposals, and ask them how they would like to proceed.

■ Summarize the key outcomes from the meeting, and end it.

This approach will make the meeting about *your adversarial peer and their key work priority* rather than the course of action you want them to adopt. It will engage your peer's interest and involvement, and should circumvent the fogging and dodging tactics that their adversarial nature might otherwise employ. This approach ought to encourage your peer to actively consider your suggestion in the light of its benefits *to their achieving their key work priority*. You might have to think on your feet in the meeting as you cannot be sure what they will claim as their key priority until they articulate it. But, having heard what that goal is, your job is to ask questions that encourage your colleague to consider how your suggested course of action will better enable them to achieve that goal. Using this process you should at the least be able to secure a hearing.

So far we have been considering a variety of one-to-one encounters with adversarial peers. Let's now explore a different peer situation, one in which a number of adversarial colleagues simultaneously cross the line and treat you in ways that you find demeaning. Consider the following case study which is set in the operations group of an engineering company.

CASE STUDY 11: GANGING UP

A talented and knowledgeable young operations manager joins an engineering firm and looks forward to learning from his more experienced colleagues. He takes his job very seriously, invests heavily in his work, and wants to provide excellent value to his new employer. His peer group are all older than him and more cynical. While they are well paid for what they do, they are less bothered than their younger peer about the quality or the integrity of the projects they undertake. They are also allies of one another, colleagues whose oppositional streak results in their ganging up on anyone they think they might be able to make wobble.

A few weeks after joining the company the younger manager is asked to work on a high-profile project alongside his peers. He decides that he will have to invest time and effort in finding ways to work effectively with a group of people he thinks he might share little in common with. The older managers are more experienced than their younger colleague, but they quickly realize that he has more up-to-date knowledge than they do, and they don't enjoy working with someone as technically able as him. However, it doesn't take the senior managers long to realize that their younger colleague is emotionally connected to his work, and that this trait results in his having a tendency to take disagreement and conflict personally. Without anyone actually putting it into words, they decide to gang up on him in peer meetings so that they can behave in ways that are uncomfortable for him, and watch him squirm.

At these times one or other of the older managers deliberately disagrees with the point of view of their younger peer, often after having specifically invited him to input to the meeting. Other managers then join in. They disagree with the younger manager on instinct, even though what he says is usually sound and well put. Nonetheless, the younger man finds himself being challenged to justify his opinion or amplify his previously comments. As he does so everyone around the table stares at him blankly and watches him redden. The young manager realizes straight away that his peers are deliberately goading him, and while he would much rather not react the way he does, he cannot help but clench his fists and start to stumble over his words. He is furious that his colleagues think it is all right to gang up on him and embarrass him. He fights his corner and what he says is always technically correct, but he feels humiliated that he cannot prevent his face from reddening and his voice from shaking.

However, his mocking colleagues continue to deride his point of view, and enjoy watching him expend energy justifying and proving his argument. Towards the end of one of these baiting sessions one of the more embittered peers waits for a period of silence and then patronizes the younger man, telling him that 'it's only work' and that he 'shouldn't take it personally.' The more that the younger manager tries to defend himself from the charge of 'taking it personally,' the more his senior colleagues smirk at him and speak patronizingly to him.

There are a number of ways in which the younger man could handle this situation. Let's explore three of them:

■ Fed up at being patronized and picked on, the younger manager contemptuously tells his peers to 'grow up.' He pushes his chair back from the table, stands up, and leaves the room. He returns to his desk, complains loudly to the people who sit near him about the conduct of 'the idiots' he has to work with, and carries on with his work. At the next and subsequent peer meetings the baiting gets worse, and on two occasions different managers actually laugh at the younger manager in front of their peers. The young manager thinks that although he is technically competent and wants to do a good job he cannot work with a group of people intent on humiliating him, and he considers resigning.

■ The younger manager takes a deep breath and knocks on the table. In the silence that ensues he tells his colleagues that their behavior demeans them not him and that he would prefer to speak with them about the way forward on the *project*. He sits very upright as he says these words, uses a firm and unwavering tone, and maintains level eye contact with each one of his colleagues in turn. He takes the view that the best way to influence this group of people toward treating him with greater respect is to shame them. Although the baiting ceases in that meeting, it does start again in subsequent meetings, although it is less frequent and less severe.

■ The younger manager stands up, moves away from the table towards the windows and rearranges the blinds in the meeting room. He then returns to the table, and while still standing upright, he tells his peers that he has been thinking about the way forward on their current joint project. He informs them that he wants to change some of the specifications for the new machinery they are installing. Then, without pausing for breath or waiting for input, and using the same clear and resolute tone, he provides them with a cogent factual analysis of the problems, pitfalls, and downsides with the existing specification on the new machinery before outlining his proposed solutions. When he has completed his presentation he looks at each person around the table one at a time, before asking if anyone would like to try to influence him toward a different point of view. No one does, and no one speaks against what he has said. He says 'That's settled then,' and unilaterally ends the meeting, saying he has other things to attend to. He leaves his adversarial peers sitting in the room in an awkward silence.

Ganging Up: Analyzing the Dynamics

Let's revisit this situation to analyze the dynamics in it. We will examine the pros and cons of the different ways of handling this situation employed by the younger manager as he seeks relief from the adversarial tactics used against him by his peer group.

In this example a young manager needs to find a way to influence his older colleagues to stop behaving in an adversarial way towards him in meetings. Their adversarial conduct is marked by a degree of childish and wayward group enmity. The young manager wants to find a way to prevent his peers from ganging up on him, and encourage them to accept that, while they might have different values from him, they can still work well together. If he succeeds in doing this he will be able to make a contribution to peer meetings without having to endure personal attacks. He might also find that he enjoys his work more, and may in time be able to influence some of his colleagues to work more conscientiously and responsibly for their employer. If he fails to influence this group of people towards treating him with greater respect, he may find that his position with the company becomes untenable, and he might have to consider leaving his employment. Let's see how he gets on.

- In the first instance, the young manager loses his temper. Fed up of being taunted in public, fed up of the unkind treatment he is receiving from older peers he could reasonably have expected to look up to, he speaks his mind openly and frankly. He tells them that he thinks they are being childish, and leaves the room in the middle of a meeting. While his reaction is understandable, it is also an unwise thing to do. He is right. His colleagues are being childish, and he can be forgiven for thinking that they are wholly in the wrong in their treatment of him. But saying so isn't going to help him. Given their adversarial nature, it will make the situation worse. They will take his premature departure from the room as encouragement to continue their inimical tactics against him. By leaving the room, even though right is on his side, the young manager unfortunately demonstrates conclusively to his colleagues that their goading gets to him and causes him to snap. This is exactly the outcome they want so, encouraged, they continue to gang up on him in future meetings. They patronize him and actually laugh at him on subsequent occasions. The young manager loses all credibility and influence with this group of people even though he is the most technically competent and knowledgeable manager in the group, and even though it is *their* behavior that is at fault, not his. By leaving the meeting so visibly upset he boxes himself into a corner. Worse still, his subsequent loud complaints about his peers in the open-plan office in which he works go against him too. It is counter-cultural in this company for one colleague to complain publicly about another, no matter what the provocation, and the colleagues who hear the young manager's complaints don't like the fact that he has broken this unwritten rule, no matter how justified he considers himself to be. As a result his reputation suffers with the people who work around him in the open-plan office, and insult is added to his injury. Overall, his handling of the situation has not done him any favors. He might consider complaining to his manager about the conduct of his peers. But it would be difficult for him to find a form of words that preserves his dignity while explaining to his boss that his peers regularly gang up on him in meetings. His boss may take the view that it is the *young manager* and not his peers who needs to do things differently. He will now have to deal with the fact that whenever one of his peers wants to have a bit of fun at his expense in the future, all he has to do is push and push until the young man reaches his snapping point again. He may even find that the baiting gets worse as the peers try to expose his snapping point sooner and faster.

■ In the second instance, the young manager confronts his peers in the meeting itself. He challenges them to cease treating him in demeaning and puerile ways. He tries to influence them toward the view that while they can gang up on him and discomfit him if they wish to, they cannot intimidate him, and should he wish it, he will be quite capable of standing up to them. He makes firm eye contact with each person in turn to denote his resolve to stand up for himself. He hopes that his self-preserving and self-respecting behavior will influence them to reduce or cease their childish games. He is partially successful, and at future meetings, the teasing does reduce in intensity and frequency, although it continues nonetheless. In this case the young manager has partially influenced the situation for the better, but he has also left himself open to further, though less provoking, instances of adversarial behavior in future. He has succeeded in putting down a marker to tell his peers that he is quite capable of drawing the line should he want to. But ideally he still needs to find a way to silence his critics fully so that he can participate in a meeting with them, confident that they will be disinclined to taunt him and he will be able to use his technical knowledge to help his employer.

■ In the third instance, the young manager has had enough. He decides to take firm action and use his technical skills and competence to strike back at his adversarial peers. He doesn't challenge them directly on their behavior toward him. Nor does he feed back to them his view that they are reducing themselves by behaving in a derisory manner. Instead, he decides to reframe the discussion around the key points the meeting has been arranged to debate. He decides that his most useful tack will be to demonstrate to his peer group that he is the most effective operations manager in the room, thereby taking control of the floor. He thinks that the real motivation behind his colleagues' desire to taunt him is their jealousy at his superior knowledge and professionalism. So he uses that very thing, his competence at his job, to strike back at them, proving conclusively to them that they need him and his input. He handles himself well. He gets up from the table while he is still being taunted and walks over to the blinds. This action wrongfoots the peers who are goading him. They expect him to remain seated and under attack. Standing up and moving away from the table regains him control of the situation, and is an unexpected turn of events as far as his peers are concerned. Then he turns the tables on them. He returns to the table and, while remaining standing, provides a thorough analysis of the pros and cons of the new machinery they are jointly installing, before outlining the changes to the specifications he proposes to solve those problems. There is nothing his colleagues can say back to him. What he has said is compelling and true. His colleagues cannot afford to disregard his views because it will backfire on them professionally if they do so. And they cannot go back to taunting him having just been presented with a clear business argument that requires their response. He has given himself a good chance of remaining on the front foot in this meeting, and there is a better than even chance that in subsequent meetings his colleagues will be disinclined to taunt him as severely as on this occasion. They may even cease to do so altogether. If they are tempted to repeat their treatment of him in future, they know that he will be able to put them in their place technically, embarrassing them into realizing that the least experienced and most junior person in the room is more on top of their joint work than they are. Using this response the young manager does a good job of calling his adversarial peers to account. He does so with minimal fuss and considerable aplomb. He will need to continue to watch out for their childish, bullying tactics again in the future, and continue to marshal his excellent technical knowledge to keep them on their toes. But, by maintaining his commitment to his own values and by using his technical competence to counter their verbal teasing, he should be able to hold his own with a particularly challenging group of adversarial peers, and avoid the prospect of having to look for alternative employment elsewhere.

This example demonstrates that, when faced with a group of adversarial colleagues prepared to cross the line and mistreat you as a group, your greatest source of influence lies in your ability to remain in the room and confront your colleagues face to face. You need to find a way of changing the focus of the conversation away from their provoking behavior and its impact on you back onto the business issues you and your peers are paid to address, and doing so by reminding the group of your skill and competence at your job will be doubly effective. While it may be tempting to leave such a potentially abusive situation, but as demonstrated in the example, leaving the room may prove to be the least effective and most damaging course of action for you. Your adversarial peers will seize on your apparent weakness with glee, and completely blind to their own shortcomings and deficiencies, may be tempted to exploit your, as they see it, character flaw in the future, pushing you harder and faster just to see what gives. Staying in a conversation with a group of adversarial peers, even ones who are ganging up on you, no matter how challenging that conversation may be, can be essential if you are to keep the dynamic between you manageable. Of course, you may decide that enough is enough and look for employment elsewhere. But if you want to keep your job and redress the balance between you and your peers, you need to find a way to confront the behavior that is offensive to you as and when it happens.

YOUR ADVERSARIAL COLLEAGUES

You may now like to take a moment to apply the lessons from this example to your own working life. You can jot down your answers to the following questions in the space below:

■ Identify a situation in which a group of adversarial peers acted together against you. Who were they, and what happened?

■ What impact did their adversarial tactics have on you and your work?

■ How did you respond at the time? To what extent was this approach successful in causing your peers to cease adopting adversarial behavior with you?

■ Looking back on it now, what else could you have done to alter the situation in your favor?

SUMMARY AND NEXT CHAPTER

This chapter has focused on a number of ways to minimize the risk involved in working with adversarial peers. The key message of the chapter has been that it is up to you to find ways of remaining in control of the process of your work when you are working with an adversarial peer. You must be prepared to change the dynamic in the relationship if you need to, so that you can get on with the tasks that sit with you while also limiting the options available to your peer to act against you. The chapter has suggested that managing your boundaries judiciously is a key self-protective tool when working with an untrustworthy and unsupportive peer. It has identified that having the courage to take action early when faced with the first evidence of adversarial intent on the part of your peer will save you a lot of frustration and grief later on. The chapter also has highlighted how framing a meeting around the key work priority of an adversarial peer can circumvent their oppositional streak, and prove particularly useful when you want to influence your peer to adopt a course of action that they oppose on instinct. The chapter has also illustrated how to turn the tables on a group of adversarial peers who are ganging up on you. It suggested that playing to a strong suit you possess, such as your technical ability, would serve you well, as well as illustrating how to avoid the pitfalls of acting out of righteous indignation at these times.

The next chapter will focus on the skills and strategies you need to employ should you find yourself managing an adversarial team member. The chapter will highlight a range of tactics that you could employ to redirect your team member's energy away from oppositional behavior towards effective performance.

CHAPTER 6

Managing an Adversarial Team Member

Confronting Counterproductive Behavior

In this chapter we will examine the dynamics of managing an adversarial team member. The chapter will explore how to identify adversarial behavior in a member of your team, as well as how to handle the issues this behavior creates for you and the other team members working for you. The chapter will examine the ins and outs of a situation in which you have organizational authority over your adversarial team member, and therefore a range of options for confronting their counterproductive behavior, but want to avoid demotivating or alienating them so that they under-perform.

The chapter will begin by examining how to manage an adversarial team member whose ambivalence adversely affects the quality of their relationships with colleagues and the tone of their input to team meetings. We will then explore how to confront an adversarial team member who is not performing effectively and who disowns their responsibility to actively try and improve their performance. We will highlight how to handle an adversarial team member whose oppositional streak results in their opposing you, their boss, on principle simply because you represent authority which they strongly dislike. The chapter will end by outlining some of the key principles to bear in mind should you want to give direct, clear feedback to an adversarial team member that their behavior has been noted, is not viewed favorably, and needs to change. We will illustrate the principles presented in the chapter with some realistic examples, and also take a look at your own experiences of working with adversarial team members.

HANDLING AN ADVERSARIAL TEAM MEMBER

The discovery that one of your team members has adversarial traits can be quite a shock. Over a period of time you might observe your team member swimming against the tide, perhaps over smaller issues and over larger ones. You might notice that their behavior affects the quality of their relationship with you and the quality of their relationships with the other people in the team. However, when you question them about their conduct, your adversarial team member expresses indignation at being pulled up, and claims to be working hard for the good of the team. The problem is that you are not sure that this is their consistent and only motivation. Perhaps you have evidence that your adversarial team member:

- Agreed to pass on a message from one of your team members to another colleague or to a client but the message didn't get through.
- Said that they would carry out a specific task that you have delegated to them – but the task didn't get done.
- Offered to complete a task for a team colleague, a task at which they excel and at which their fellow team member doesn't perform effectively – but then the task didn't get done well or at all.

Any of these instances would be quite understandable if your adversarial team member:

- Was rushed off their feet.
- Genuinely forgot to attend to the relevant task.
- Made an honest mistake.
- Suddenly had to drop everything and handle a high-priority item instead.

But, in none of the cases you have observed is this the way of it. Rather, you suspect that their failure to deliver is quite purposeful. You think it could be a choice, even if it is a subconscious choice, and one that they subsequently disown when questioned about it. You think there could be a pattern to their behavior, a pattern that results in them deliberately failing to do certain things, commit to certain courses of action, or execute against certain tasks, simply because they want to act in this way. Consider the following example.

CASE STUDY 12: PROVOKING DISAGREEMENT

A team of eight full-time consultants in a PR consultancy report to an experienced and astute manager. She is an able leader and well thought of in the firm. She manages her team members through a mixture of one-to-one meetings and a fortnightly team briefing to which all eight members of her team are invited. The purpose of the team briefing is to make decisions about the future direction of the team's largest accounts, and for the team members to appraise one another about sales activity they have undertaken during the previous fortnight. The tone of these meetings is cordial and characterized by a high degree of listening. This is partly due to the example set by the team leader, but also due to the way in which the team members usually handle one another.

The team leader decides to use the last half of one particular team briefing to decide on an agenda for the upcoming offsite team briefing. Towards the end of the meeting the team reaches consensus and agrees that a good use of the offsite briefing would be to look for performance improvements around sales and marketing activity. At this precise moment, one member of the team makes a surprising interjection. Interrupting the colleague seated on his left while she is still speaking, this team member puts forward the view that the offsite briefing should not focus on sales and marketing activity as had just been agreed, but ought instead to focus on team development issues. The team member putting forward this point of view expands on his reasoning for several minutes before drawing breath. As a result of his input the team briefing runs over by 20 minutes, as the team debate the issues he has raised. Eventually, the team decide to stick with their original plan and use the offsite briefing to examine improvements to their approach to sales and marketing activity.

Sadly, at every team briefing thereafter this team member does exactly the same thing. Towards the end of the meeting, at a point when agreement has been reached on an important issue, he interjects and puts forward an alternative point of view. On each occasion that he does this, the team members then spend upwards of 20 minutes debating the issues, before more often than not arriving back where they started by adopting the original decision. The team leader grows tired of what she sees as a futile waste of the team's time, and determines to speak with this team member during her next one-to-one meeting with him.

Provoking Disagreement: Analyzing the Dynamics

Let's revisit this scenario to analyze the dynamics in it and explore the ins and outs of the situation. In this scenario a team leader grows tired of what she sees as one of her team members wasting the time of the team by misjudging when to put forward an alternative point of view. To her mind, this team member leaves his interjections too late, a state of affairs which results in the team meeting often running over time as it tries to accommodate his wish to debate an alternative point of view. The team leader thinks that the quite lengthy discussions, which follow this team member's poorly timed input, don't achieve anything concrete. Her view is that they needlessly take the meeting off track, only for it to return to where it was before he created the diversion.

However, the team leader hasn't really understood the motivation of her team member. She thinks that he takes his time to form a view, needs to reflect before coming to a conclusion, and likes to listen to all the arguments before determining what view he wants to put forward. She thinks that these features of what she would describe as his work style account for why he so often makes late interjections to meetings. By ascribing these benign motives to him she misses the point. In fact, he is quite quick to form a view, and usually arrives at the meeting already having decided what point of view he wants to put forward in it. The issue is not that he takes his time to form an opinion. It is that he chooses to give his opinion at the precise moment at which the team has reached a consensus, and that his opinion is always in direct opposition to that prevailing view. Let's take a closer look at what he is actually doing.

This team member has a high need for control, an oppositional streak, and an adversarial mindset. These combined factors mean that, while he can be a productive and resourceful member of the team, he also wants to kick out at the team from time and time and remind its members that he is there. He chooses to do this in team meetings when everyone will have to listen to him, and he times his input to try to destroy consensus and agreement in the group. He picks his moments carefully, and when he speaks, he disagrees with or objects to a decision which the team has just made, offering an alternative and contradictory way forward instead. His input usually takes the form of an opinion rather than a presentation of a new fact. He then speaks for several minutes, expounding his point of view and explaining why his newly stated ideas ought to hold sway. His interjections are usually greeted with silence by his colleagues who, out of politeness, feel compelled to listen to his argument.

The team dynamic is characterized by a high degree of listening, which results in the team members, no matter how fed up they are with their colleague, listening to him and subsequently debating his ideas. What then ensues is a 20 to 30 minute discussion about the pros and cons of the oppositional team member's new idea versus the pros and cons of the consensus view to which he objected. The tone of these discussions is usually increasingly fractious and irritated. The team members spend time discussing the ins and outs of the new suggestion, going over old ground, reiterating previously considered arguments and comparing them with the new one. Often the original decision is adopted anyway, albeit after a delay. Sometimes the meeting runs out of time, leaving some colleagues late for their next meeting, and sometimes the manager has to end the meeting before the discussion is concluded. On these occasions she invariably makes the decision, and usually adopts the original point of view.

What the team manager doesn't realize is that her team member doesn't interject over issues that divide the meeting, only over issues on which the meeting agrees. It is as if the fact that everyone agrees *is* the trigger for his objection. In this sense, he wants to destroy the rapport between his colleagues and undermine the agreement in the room, taking the meeting down a route he determines simply to give him a spurious sense of control. If his manager handles his behavior treating it as an issue of timing rather than as an issue related to his adversarial nature, she would find it increasingly difficult to confront him and secure the kind of behavior change she wants to see. We will revisit this scenario later in the chapter to see how she gets on when she tackles him.

THE SIGNALS OF AN ADVERSARIAL TEAM MEMBER

We have just explored an example in which an adversarial team deliberately disagrees with his team colleagues. He does this to destroy consensus in the team as a prelude to taking control of the meeting. His actions are motivated by his need to:

- Provoke dissent.
- Block progress.
- Thwart his manager and his team colleagues.
- Control the meeting.

The signals that the conduct of one of your team members is adversarial may be quite subtle as in this scenario, and consequently could be open to misinterpretation. Your adversarial team member may be brazen enough to come straight out with it and declare their antagonism towards you or their team colleagues, in which case the issues will be on the table and it will be up to you as team leader to decide how to handle them. But it is much more likely that your adversarial team member will handle things in a more understated and delicate way, one which means that you could misjudge their motivation, ascribing to it a more benign motive than is actually warranted. You might quite rightly decide that something is amiss, but misunderstand what is actually going on.

It is these more subtle instances of adversarial conduct that are the trickiest to handle, and the ones that can take up the most management time. If you take the issues at face value, as the team leader in the above scenario does, then you might fail to bring about the kind of behavior change you want. You could end up having quite lengthy conversations about the behavior you want to see altered, conversations which will result in your team member:

- Justifying their approach.
- Pointing out the benefits of their way of doing things.
- Highlighting the deficiencies of their colleagues' approaches.
- Changing the impetus of the conversation away from their behavior onto something else such as your, as they see, erroneous perceptions about them.
- Failing to take your feedback on board and continuing to use the counter-productive behavior.

In these cases you could end up wasting time, becoming frustrated, and achieving little or nothing. To bring about the change in attitude and consequent change in behavior that you want, you need to address the underlying oppositional streak in your team member, and do so in a way that motivates them to address their intrapersonal issues. And to do this you need to use a form of words that holds your team member directly accountable for their oppositional behavior, as we will see shortly when we return to the scenario we have been discussing.

DODGING THE ISSUE

Those of you who have already confronted an adversarial team member over their behavior may know just how challenging a task this can be. Your adversarial colleague may well be quite adept at:

- Dodging the issue.

- Creating fog around the issues.
- Turning the tables on you and blaming you for the situation they find themselves in.

If you confront your team member directly over, say, their failure to complete a specific task on time, they may tell you that they forgot to do the task and will get to it straightaway, when in fact they didn't do it because they didn't want to and are now fobbing you off. Or they may turn on you and claim that you are putting them under undue pressure, that you are always on their case, or that you are being unreasonably demanding and pressurizing of them. They may sound so genuinely aggrieved that you may even wonder if there is truth to some of these characterizations of you. It is only when you confront the underlying adversarial intent in clear and simple language that you will be able to hold your adversarial colleague accountable. Let's return to the example set in the PR consultancy and see what happens when the team leader decides to talk with her adversarial team member about his conduct in team briefing meetings.

CASE STUDY 13: CONFRONTATION

After a series of team briefings in which her troublesome team member makes time consuming late interjections, the team leader decides that she must confront him. She does so during her next one-to-one meeting with him. After raising two initial issues that she wants to put to him, she tells her adversarial team member that she has something important that she wants to discuss with him. There are a number of ways in which the team leader could handle this part of her interview with her team member. Let's examine three of them.

- The team leader tells her team member that she has noticed that he has a habit of bringing up important issues late in team briefings, and that as a result of his late comments a number of briefings have overrun. Before she can add anything else, her team member interrupts her. He says that he is glad she has brought up this particular subject because he wants to have a word with her about the quality of debate at the team briefings. He then tells her that he thinks some of the discussions at the meeting are long-winded, and asks her whether she has any suggestions for making the meeting more pertinent and less digressive.
- The team leader tells her team member that she is concerned at

the number of times that he brings up key issues after a decision has been made rather than before it has been made, and that she would prefer he made his suggestions earlier in the team briefing meeting. The team member says that he would if he could, but he thinks that the meeting format could be improved. He then spends two minutes speaking about suggested changes he would recommend to the meeting, before saying that he has an important client call to make and would like to reschedule the rest of the one-to-one for another time.

■ The team leader sits upright in her chair and tells her team member that she wants him to input to team briefings in a timely manner, or if fails to do so, to abide by the decision of the meeting. Speaking in a paced manner and maintaining level eye contact with him throughout, she says that she won't allow him to reopen closed discussions in future, and that, as far as she is concerned, if he decides to object after a decision has been made, it will be too late for the objection to be debated. She then says that while he has some useful things to say in team briefings, she thinks that his failure to work with the meeting is affecting his reputation in her eyes and in the eyes of the team as a whole. She ends by saying that she would like to see him react constructively to her comments, and not use them as an opportunity to become obstructive or oppositional. Then she asks him to respond and waits quietly until he does so.

Confrontation: Analyzing the Dynamics

Let's revisit this scenario to analyze the impact of the three alternative ways that the team leader handles the confrontation. We will explore the ins and outs of each way of handling it to identify why they produce such different responses in the team member.

In this example the team leader decides to sit down with her errant team member and get to the bottom of his irritating habit of taking the team briefing off course late on. Her aim in having this confrontation is to encourage her team member toward changing his behavior, and either giving his input before a decision has been reached, or alternatively abiding by the consensus in the room rather than trying to revisit the issue. She hopes that she can encourage an otherwise resourceful and capable team member to use his considerable skills constructively for the good of the team, rather than continue to upset the process of team meetings. Let's take a look at how she gets on. We will examine the different ways in which she puts her points to the team member, and analyze his responses back to her. We will do this to see what we can learn about the dynamic between them as well as the nature of his adversarial mindset.

- In the first instance, the team leader approaches the confrontation as a collaborative discussion. She assumes that goodwill exists between her and her team member, and takes it for granted that he will respond in kind to her offer of a mutual exploration of the issues she wants to raise. She starts the discussion by saying conversationally that she thinks he has got into the bad habit of giving his input to the team briefing too late on, and that as a result of this some of the team briefings have overrun. She draws breath and is completely unprepared for the speed with which he jumps in and takes over. He goes onto the front foot immediately, switching the focus of the discussion and its subject matter in an instant. He tells his manager that he is pleased she has brought this subject up. He tells her that he thinks some of the team briefings are full of waffle, and asks her what ideas she has to remedy the situation. In one sentence he has turned the tables on his boss, putting her on the back foot and making her management of the team briefing the problem, rather than his own oppositional behavior in it. His boss is unprepared for this tactic and is thrown by it. She takes it seriously and tries to reply to it, effectively enabling him to wriggle off the hook as she struggles to justify her handling of the meeting rather than hold him accountable for his behavior in it. He has bamboozled her, and to good effect.
- In the second instance, the team leader is more direct. She tells her team member that she is concerned at how frequently he brings up important issues *after* a decision has been made rather than before it has been made, and says that she would rather he said what he wants to say before a decision is taken. Her team member responds by saying that he would if he could, but he can't because of the way the meeting is formatted. He then speaks for fully two minutes about the various issues he perceives with the format of the meeting, before outlining how he would like to address them. He succeeds in making a number of valid points, points that do indeed highlight improvement opportunities with the meeting. But rather than introduce this material for honest reasons, the team member does so to cloud the issues his manager has put to him. He creates an effective smokescreen because he manages to speak

for so long, and because what he has to say is genuinely interesting. The problem is that he doesn't want to stay in the room and hear his boss's feedback on his ideas. Instead he creates a second smokescreen by claiming that he has an urgent client call to make, one he had somehow omitted to mention beforehand and one which he 'realizes' he now has to make without receiving a text, phone call or pager message to inform him about it. He exits the room leaving his manager with much to think through. She has to decide what changes if any she will make to the format of the meeting following her team member's feedback, whether the format really is the issue behind his late interjections at the team briefing, and whether she hasn't just been duped by his supposed urgent client call. Only if his behavior doesn't change after she makes her changes to the team-briefing format will she be able to confront him a second time, ideally using a more effective approach than this time. The team member has bought himself some more time and sent his boss on a detour, but may well be held to account at a future date.

▪ In the third instance, the team manager is both clever and effective in her confrontation with her team member. She doesn't fall into the trap of assuming goodwill. Nor does she allow her team member to create a smokescreen, interrupt her, or change the focus of the meeting away from the issues she wants to discuss with him to something else of his choosing. She retains control of the meeting throughout, saying everything she wants to say before ceasing speaking and requiring him to respond. The team leader starts the confrontation by telling her team member that she wants him to either input to team briefing discussions before a decision is made, or abide by the decision without commenting further on it. She tells him that she will not allow him to re-open issues that have already been subject to a decision, and that if he tries to do so in future, she will not allow the points he has raised to be debated. So far, she has presented him with an ultimatum, a choice based on her authority as team leader and her requirements of him as a member of her team. He can either provide his input early or not at all, but he cannot do what he has always done and re-open closed issues after a decision has been made. The team leader makes these comments using an authoritative tone. She is the team leader and if she says that is how it must be, then that is how it must be. Her usual style is much more participative than this, and the team member realizes that this is a conversation he needs to take seriously. But she hasn't finished yet. She then tells him that while she thinks he does have some good points to make in team briefings, she also thinks that his failure to work with the meeting is resulting in his reputation being tarnished in the eyes of his team colleagues, and in her eyes too. This comment really hits home. His reputation matters to him, and the team member doesn't like the idea that his conduct at team briefings is causing his colleagues and manager to think less well of him. In fact, being informed by his boss that there is a direct connection between his behavior and his reputation taking a hit is uncomfortable for him. The team manager lets these words sink in, then completes her input by telling her team member that she would like to think that he will react constructively to her comments and not become oppositional or obstructive. These last comments are particularly well judged by the team leader. She makes her view of his conduct explicit by using the words 'oppositional' and 'obstructive,' and this makes it very difficult for him to act in either way. She effectively unmasks him and leaves him unable to resort to either tactic again, either in this meeting or in the team briefing. She ends the confrontation by asking him for his reaction to what she has said, and waits patiently until he finds something to say. He may well say 'Of course I won't be obstructive,' or 'I have never been obstructive,' or some such. But whatever he says at this awkward moment for him, she has called his bluff, and it is very unlikely that he will be foolish enough to repeat his unproductive conduct at future team briefings.

Having spent some time analyzing the characteristics of ineffective and effective confrontations with adversarial team members, we will now examine in more detail why the third approach, that of naming the game, is such an effective tactic to use.

NAMING THE GAME

When the team leader tells her team member that she expects him to react constructively to her comments, and not to resort to either oppositional or obstructive behavior, she 'names the game.' She puts into words the exact attitudes and behaviors that her team member uses which are so annoying for her and so unhelpful for the process of team briefings. And she unmasks his adversarial game. She lets him know that she is on to him, that she sees through his control game, and that she expects it to stop. Although she doesn't say it in so many words, he can be left in no doubt that she will be prepared to act should he try this particular tactic in the future.

This approach leaves the team member with nowhere to go. Although he won't say so, his behavior will change from that point onwards. He won't use ambivalent or oppositional behavior in front of this boss in her team briefings in the future. He won't risk the consequences he knows will be his should he try it on again. And he will make his comments before decisions are made, or not at all, if he wants to play an active role in the team and preserve the positive reputation he has built. But why does 'naming the game' result in behavior change?

When you 'name the game' with one of your adversarial team members you change the dynamic between you completely. Even though your team member won't say so and might not even reveal their discomfort facially or through other non-verbal signals, they suddenly realize that they do not have the degree of control they thought they had over you, and cannot dupe you. They are faced with a stark choice: use the behavior again and risk being embarrassed when you call them on their choice of tactics publicly, or cease using the behavior at all. Almost all of your team members will cease using the counter-productive behavior. Should any of them try to outwit you and use it again even after you have warned them, all you need do is remind them of your previous conversation with them in the same firm, clear tone. It is a highly effective way of confronting adversarial behavior in a team member.

YOUR ADVERSARIAL COLLEAGUES

You might like to consider your own team and its adversarial members. Answer the following questions and jot down your response to each of them in the spaces below:

■ Identify a team member whom you think might display adversarial traits. What does this colleague say or do which leads you to regard them as adversarial?

■ What impact does this behavior have on you and their other team colleagues?

■ In what ways have you sought to confront this team member over their behavior?

■ How effective has this approach been at encouraging your team member to cease using adversarial behavior?

■ Should you need to address a similar situation in the future, how would you handle the issues?

So far, we have been discussing examples in which an adversarial team member uses counter-productive behavior, behavior which is about gaining a degree of elicit control over the team meetings they attend while also signaling their opposition to their manager and co-workers. But what about a different situation, one in which your team member manages to keep their oppositional streak under check until something specific happens which causes them to rebel? Consider the following example.

CASE STUDY 14: REBEL MODE

A newly qualified accountant accepts a probationary role in a team of tax advisers in a large accountancy firm. She is thrilled to be offered employment in a household-name company, and quickly establishes a reputation as someone who is dedicated, conscientious, and technically able. After three months her manager, the head of tax, makes her appointment permanent. He sits her down to talk through his perceptions of her first quarter with the firm and to provide her with feedback on her performance. The meeting goes very well, and the newly qualified accountant leaves it believing that she is working for a manager who is supportive towards her and who thinks well of her.

However, over the next four months she finds her work increasingly onerous, in terms of both workload and the complexity of the tax matters she is asked to handle. Her boss is also very busy but makes time for her whenever he can. He notes that she is slow to ask for help, so he makes a point of arranging meetings to enquire how she is getting on, and to offer assistance should she want it. Her responses at these times are often diffident, as if she doesn't welcome his interest, and the meetings are invariably over quite quickly.

A few weeks after the latest of these short meetings, when he observes her looking particularly tired one Monday morning, the head of tax forms the view that his newest team member is beginning to struggle with the responsibilities she has on her desk. Keen to respond supportively, he walks over to her desk, asks her how she is getting on, and is surprised at the ferocity with which she asserts that she is fine. On two other occasions over the next month the boss asks her how she is finding her work, and on both occasions she shrugs off his enquiry briskly.

Two weeks later the team member makes a series of mistakes which come to the attention of her boss and one of the clients on whose behalf she is acting. Although the head of tax handles the incident as tactfully as he can, this episode marks a change in his relationship with his team member. From then on she behaves differently towards him. She is truculent, chippy, and awkward to deal with. Never rude enough for him to openly confront her, she is nonetheless a less courteous and less effective employee than she had been before this incident. On two occasions the head of tax sits her down to review her progress, and on each occasion she is largely silent, contributes little to the meeting, and is visibly relieved when he draws it to a close.

Her manager struggles to interpret her behavior, and forms the view that she is no longer comfortable working for the tax team. He asks her if she would like to move on secondment elsewhere in the company to get a flavor for other departments in the firm. Her response, that she is working flat out and is offended at his suggestion that she isn't pulling her weight, baffles him, as it doesn't address the point he put to her at all. Over the next week his team member becomes increasingly stroppy with her peer group, and two of them complain to him about her conduct. Two days later she comments to the office manager that she is doing so much work at home that she will need to 'steal some paper' to restock her own supplies. The office manager relates the conversation to the head of tax, who reacts with justifiable anger.

Rebel Mode: Analyzing the Dynamics

Let's revisit this scenario to examine its dynamics and explore the ins and outs of the situation it describes. In it a newly qualified accountant accepts a probationary role in a major accountancy firm, and initially does very well. She is clearly able, and establishes both liking and respect with her peer group and her boss, the head of tax. She regards her boss as both supportive towards her and someone who thinks positively about her, a combination that goes down very well with her and initially brings out the best in her. She does well during her first three months with the firm, and her probationary role is made permanent.

But, as her workload increases and the nature of the tax matters she is charged with becomes more complex, the new employee begins to struggle. Her supportive boss enquires how she is getting on, and is surprised that she doesn't want to discuss her workload or her apparent difficulties with it. However, he keeps an eye on her, and when he notices her looking particularly tired a few weeks later, he opens up a conversation with her about her progress. He is taken aback by the ferocity with which she asserts that she is fine. He gets the clear message that his interest is not welcomed by his team member, and he desists.

However, when she starts to make mistakes in her work he can no longer play it her way. He has to intervene, and even though he does so tactfully, his relationship with his employee doesn't recover. From that moment on she becomes difficult to deal with. She is quarrelsome and fractious. Never openly defiant either with him or with her peer group, she is nonetheless sullen and surly, and difficult to be around. She makes it quite clear to her manager that she does not value any sort of interaction with him, and refuses to give any input when he arranges two separate one-to-one meetings with her. Eventually, having formed a view that she doesn't like working in the tax department and might benefit from a change of scene, her boss asks her if she would like to leave the department, and is amazed at her reaction, a vigorous assertion that she is working flat out. He is thrown by the fact that she doesn't address the specific point he puts to her, and instead seems to take his suggestion as a slight on her industriousness. Once more he desists, and lets her return to her work. Shortly afterwards she comments to the office manager that she wants to 'steal some paper' to restock her shelves at home, a comment which infuriates her boss when the office manager tells him about it. What has happened in the mind of this team member that results in someone apparently well-adjusted, hard working, and talented descending into an adversarial spiral? Let's take a look.

As long as things go well for the newly qualified accountant she is a sunny and constructive member of staff. Initially, this is certainly the case. Her probationary period is a big success, and as a result her employment is made permanent. She establishes a positive working relationship with her boss, who, at this stage is someone she enjoys working for. She believes correctly that he is well disposed towards her, approves of her, and enjoys having her in the department. And this is the crux of the matter. This employee is not that mature, no matter how well she presents herself outwardly. Deep down she has a high need for approval, especially approval from an authority figure such as her boss. As long as she believes that her boss thinks well of her and her work she will be sunny side up. She will be a productive and engaged member of the team. But as soon as she starts to fear that her boss no longer holds her in high esteem, she will become edgy, obstreperous, and sulky, depending on how much approval she believes she has lost. And this is exactly what happens. From the moment her errors affect her client work, and even though her boss handles the situation tactfully, she fears she has lost his approval, and her conduct becomes more and more counterproductive.

Whether her boss does in fact make a drastic reappraisal of her based on her making a series of mistakes is not the issue. The issue is her *perception* that he might. She comes to believe that her boss thinks considerably less well of her than he did when he hired her, and she cannot handle the conflict this creates for her. She needs his approval, and she thinks she has lost the better part of it. She begins to mishear his innocent enquiries about how she is getting on as undermining insinuations that she isn't doing very well. She fails to realize that he has her best interests at heart in his handling of her errors, and doesn't notice the tact with which he manages the situation. Instead she worries that her boss has, as she sees, seen through her, and now thinks that she isn't as competent as he first thought. She doesn't hear any of his offers of support or input as development opportunities, instead seeing them as meetings at which her lack of competence might be exposed. She refuses the very offers of help she needs. She doesn't have an adult conversation with the boss about her projects or her progress. She doesn't take up his offer of helping her manage an onerous workload. She doesn't ask him how he thinks she is doing, or what else he would like to see from her. She doesn't admit to herself that she is struggling and could do with some input. Instead she pushes away her supportive boss in the very meetings he sets up to offer her support, and leaves herself isolated and over-worked. Her mistrust of him is self-defeating and she fast approaches full-on rebel mode.

For his part, he boss notices her changed persona and attributes it incorrectly to her being unhappy in the department. He doesn't see her altered mental state as a product of her fear that she has lost his approval and good regard. It doesn't occur to him that such a dynamic exists in their relationship. Nor does he realize just how sensitive her approval radar is for perceived changes in his attitude to her and her work. He thinks that a change of scene will be good for this employee, and suggests that she might like to move to another part of the firm. This suggestion feeds the young accountant's fears that she has lost his approval. She hears this suggestion as a clear signal that he doesn't want her working in the department any more. Her reaction is furious. She tells him that she is working flat out, in a tone of voice designed to convey her anger that he might be characterizing her as slacker he wants to get rid of, something that hasn't crossed his mind. Her actions demonstrate just how much she listens to her internal fears, how poor a judge of character she is, how little she trusts her boss, and how little she actually hears what he is saying to her.

Eventually, she can no longer hide her growing opposition to her manager and her employer. She moves from pushing her boss away to behaving badly with her peers. She becomes stroppy with her colleagues, two of whom complain about her. Then she unwisely comments that she needs to 'steal some paper' from her employer to make up for the paper she has used at home. Whether she actually means 'steal' as opposed to 'replace' is a moot point. Her choice of words reveals her hostility towards her employer, hostility which moves from latent to active when she thinks that her boss no longer approves of her and wants her to leave the department.

In the space of a few short weeks she tumbles from being a productive, enthusiastic member of staff into a confrontational, adversarial member of staff, one who speaks openly about pilfering from her employer, who is rude to co-workers, and who expresses considerable enmity towards her trustworthy and supportive manager.

ANTAGONISM TOWARDS AUTHORITY

In the above example an employee moves from being a productive and effective member of the team to being a crabby and irascible member of the team in a few short months. She ends up displaying a series of traits characteristic of an adversarial employee who carries a level of antagonism towards authority. In her case her antagonism is aimed at two sources of authority: her boss, the head of the tax department, and her employer, the accountancy firm. She is uncooperative towards her boss, pushes him away, ascribes inappropriate motives to his innocent words of support, and refuses to work with him when he tries to help her. She lets her antagonism towards authority extend to her employer too. She is rude to her employer's other staff, so much so that two of them make complaints about her conduct. Then she speaks openly in the office about her wish to 'steal some paper' from the firm. While it would be true to say that she displays an alarming lack of judgment in allowing her petulant side such free rein at work, it is also true to say that she has little insight into her own behavior. What could account for her words and actions?

This employee simultaneously fears authority and needs approval from an authority figure, in this case her manager. She has a higher than usual need to feel approved of by an authority figure, even when she makes mistakes and gets things wrong, a need that drives much of her behavior at work. As long as she believes that she has the approval of her boss she works hard for him, and in this mode she is genuinely engaged and productive, someone who establishes liking and respect, someone who is open and bright around the office. But, as soon as fears that she has lost some or all of her boss's approval, or fears she might be about to lose it, her fragile self-esteem starts to crumble and she becomes destructive to herself and her workplace relationships.

Her definition of what constitutes an impending loss of approval centers on her manager's attitude to her and her work. Not being that able interpersonally, and lacking both the skills and maturity she needs to remain in a conversation about her progress with her boss, she regularly misinterprets him. She puts a spin on his words that he doesn't intend. She pushes him away. She mishears what he says to her. And each time she does one of these things, she closes down an opportunity to realize that, even though she is making mistakes and things are not going that well for her, he hasn't lost faith in her. In fact he wants to support her and help her through a difficult time at work. This remains the case even when she makes a series of mistakes that affect her work for a client. But sadly she cannot see past her own internal agenda and her own fears, and she comes to believe that she has had it in his eyes, and that there is no way back for her. Her mind moves into rebel mode, and she becomes oppositional towards both her employer and her manager, feels anger towards them both, and takes advantage of opportunities to work against them.

This is a particularly self-destructive dynamic in the young accountant because anyone who behaves so poorly at work will inevitably incur the disfavor of her peers and her manager. And this is exactly what happens. Initially two peers complain about her, which is bad enough, but not the pivotal issue. That comes shortly afterwards when her manager reacts with anger on being told that she has made a comment about stealing paper from the firm. At this point she does risk losing the approval of her manager, but only at this point. She risks losing his approval as a direct result of publicly speaking about stealing paper from the firm, and for no other reason. Depending on how he handles this situation, she may or may come to see the truth of the matter: that during the period of time in which she becomes more and more difficult to deal with, she actually retains her boss's good regard, and that she only risks losing it when her rebellious and adversarial mindset cause her to step over the line and suggest that she might thieve from her employer.

Those of you who work with a team member who displays similar strongly adversarial traits to the young accountant may recognize the self-destructive spiral described in this scenario. You may regard your querulous and difficult team member as someone who demonstrates a degree of antagonism towards you as an authority figure. So, how do you manage this member of staff, someone who opposes you because you are the very thing you are employed to be: an authority figure? Let's return to the action and see how the tax manager handles the situation.

CASE STUDY 15: GENEROUS SPIRIT

After a series of damaging incidents in which his newly qualified team member falls publicly from grace, the head of tax decides to sit down with her and talk through the issues her behavior is causing for him and for her. He telephones her to arrange an urgent meeting with her, a meeting which he tells her is to review her conduct during a number of recent incidents around the office. He tells her that the meeting will take precedence over all other work on her desk, and that he expects her in his office at two o'clock that afternoon.

When she walks into his office he asks her to sit. Then he begins the meeting. He starts by saying that he would like to use the time to encourage her to step back from her day-to-day work and get her bearings. He says that her work during her first three months was commendable, that since then her workload has become more complicated and onerous, and that he has tried many times to offer her support and mentoring as and when he has seen her struggling. At this point the young accountant opens her mouth to interject, but her boss holds up his hand to signal that the floor is his. He continues by saying that he is aware that things have not gone well for her recently. He cites the two complaints made about her by her peers, and what he terms the 'unfortunate incident' surrounding her comments about wanting to steal office paper. Then, without pausing, he says that he would like to draw a line under the whole episode and move on.

He watches the reaction on the face of his young team member and then says that he wants her to leave his office with a positive outlook and a determination to succeed that has been lacking of late. He says that he will be asking a senior tax manager to mentor her for the next three months, and that he expects her to make good use of his time. He says he will be touching base with her mentor at regular intervals, and that she will report directly to her mentor and not to him. He ends the meeting by telling her that he will speak with her again at the end of the three-month period to assess her progress. Then he signals that the meeting is over, and opens the door so that she can leave.

Generous Spirit: Analyzing the Dynamics

Let's revisit this scenario to examine the dynamics and explore the ins and outs of the situation it describes. In it the head of tax, fed up at the conduct of his talented but wayward team member, decides to act decisively to end the self- destructive cycle she has got herself into. He acts out of a sense that she has much to offer, that she can amend her ways if handled in the right way, and because he is a generous man who doesn't want a promising career to be ruined if he can prevent it.

The head of tax calls a meeting with his team member, a meeting that he wants to keep short and at which he alone will speak. He makes it clear to her that she will attend the meeting and that it will be in his office. By setting the meeting up this way, he uses his authority to set out the ground rules for the meeting, a meeting at which he requires her attendance. When she arrives he asks her to sit. He does not ask her how she is, or engage in any chitchat. He simply begins.

He tells her that he sees the meeting as an opportunity for her to take stock and reappraise her situation. Then, without waiting for her to reply, he carries straight on using the same understated, clear, factual style. He tells her that her first three months with the firm went very well. But as he observed her workload and projects becoming more difficult to manage, he tried many times to offer her help and support as and when he saw her struggling. He refuses the young accountant the option of interjecting at this point and moves on to his next point. He says that he is aware that things have not gone well for her recently. He cites the two complaints made by her peers, and refers to her unfortunate comments about wanting to steal office paper. Then, without pausing, he says that he would like to draw a line under the whole episode and move on.

The young accountant is stunned. She was expecting, at the very least, a severe dressing down, but instead has been given a lifeline. Her boss notes her startled expression but simply keeps going, giving her neither the time nor the opportunity to do anything but listen to him. He tells her that he wants her to leave his office with a renewed outlook. He says he wants to see her demonstrate a determination to succeed, something which has not been evident in her conduct of late. He tells her that he will arrange for her to be assigned to a mentor for a period of three months, and that he will be checking on her progress with her mentor on a regular basis. Finally, he says that he will expect to meet with her again after three months and see where she has got to. Then he ends the meeting and opens the door so she can leave his office.

Throughout the entire interview the young accountant does not speak, but when she leaves, her attitude has changed. She is no longer in rebel mode. She is no longer adversarial towards either her manager or her employer. And she is no longer antagonistic towards her boss or his authority. She wants to succeed, and is determined to try to turn around her reputation in the firm. She doesn't say any of this, but her boss knows it. How can such a significant change have been affected in such a short meeting, especially one in which she does not speak?

The head of tax is nothing if not astute. He hires the young accountant because he believes in her ability, and even when she appears to be struggling early on in her permanent employment he keeps faith in her. He thinks she has something to offer, and being an able mentor and supportively minded, he does not want to give up on someone he believes has the makings of an effective and productive accountant. However, he has also observed her adversarial nature, and is not at all pleased at her disloyalty to her employer or her rudeness to her colleagues around the office. He uses his knowledge of her and her character to craft a short, sharp, effective meeting at which to confront her over her conduct and set her on the road to recovery from her antagonism towards authority.

The head of tax creates a space in which to present the young accountant with a succinct, factual description of her time at the accountancy firm, one that includes all the highs and all the lows. He does not shirk his responsibility to call it like it is. He quite fairly and properly begins by commending her on the quality of her work during her probationary period. But then he refers to her recent struggle, her refusal to accept his offer of supportive input, her rudeness to her colleagues, and her comments about stealing from her employer. It is key to what he is about to do next that his summary of her time with the firm includes everything, warts and all.

By giving a full and frank account of her time with the firm in a low-key factual style, the head of tax conveys to the accountant that the meeting is being conducted against a backdrop of truth. And the truth is that she has had more lows than highs in recent weeks. He makes it clear that he will neither water down how poor some of her behavior has been, nor overlook the damage it has done to her credibility. He calls a spade a spade. He deliberately characterizes her recent workload as a 'struggle,' and won't allow her to try to gainsay this description. He doesn't even let her speak, but raises his palm towards her and prevents her from complaining about his choice of word or trying to present her conduct in an alternative and less damaging light. He retains absolute control of the meeting. His description of her time with the firm is both fair and accurate, and deep down she knows it. She doesn't try to interrupt again. There is nothing she can really say. She is in the room with an authority figure who does not conform to her image of authority, and it renders her mute. He isn't unfair to her. He doesn't abuse his position over her. He isn't unkind to her. He doesn't use anger to make his points, nor does he belittle her. He doesn't lie or distort the truth about her. He doesn't even signal any disapproval of her, despite the fact that she has given him ample opportunity and much ammunition to do so should he wish. Instead, despite everything she has said and done, he offers her a second chance. It is this generosity of spirit that causes her to have a change of heart. She is truly, silently changed.

He tells her that he wants to draw a line under everything and hopes she will leave the room with her right head on. He doesn't tell her off, threaten her, or suggest that she pull her socks up. He merely says that he would like to think she would change her approach on leaving the room. He gives her a choice: go out there and succeed. Or don't. Then he gives her a source of support to help her succeed in the form of an experienced tax adviser who will act as her mentor for the next three months. And she chooses. She leaves the room a changed woman; having said nothing in the meeting and done nothing except had an encounter with good authority in the person of the head of tax.

At one stroke he dismantles her ambivalence towards authority by being none of the things she fears he might be. At one stroke he alters the dynamic between them, thereby altering the dynamic within her, and she leaves the meeting no longer at war with herself, him, or her employer. It is his genuinely generous spirit that enables him to achieve this outcome with such economy of effort and in such a short period of time. He is genuinely supportive towards her, and continues to believe in her even though her conduct really doesn't deserve it. He notes her internal conflicts and ambivalences but sees past them to the able young accountant inside her, the young accountant who does want to succeed if only she could see past her own self-destructive tendencies.

Only time will tell whether the accountant will take advantage of her second chance, but at least she does now have an opportunity to turn around her reputation in the firm, thanks to the generosity of her manager.

GIVING FEEDBACK TO AN ADVERSARIAL TEAM MEMBER

We have been exploring an example in which a manager genuinely believes in the ability of one of his staff, doesn't want her to fail, and decides to address her adversarial nature in an act of generosity. It is a calculated gamble on his part, one he is only prepared to take because he has faith in her talent and believes that given the right encouragement she will be able to rise above her antagonistic mindset and act more maturely. It is a choice he can make because of his inner belief in her and his big-hearted spirit. And in this instance, it has a good chance of succeeding.

However, this approach isn't for everyone. You may feel disinclined to handle your adversarial team member in this way. You may decide that you cannot, hand on heart, demonstrate generosity towards your team member for any number of valid reasons. Instead you want to provide them with clear, behaviorally based feedback on their conduct and let them sort it out. So how do you address the counterproductive behavior displayed by an adversarial team member in a more conventional way and still succeed in bringing about behavior change?

Those of you who want to go down this route need to:

- Identify a specific incident around which to build your feedback.
- Prepare a full, accurate, factual description of what you observed your team member say and do that was counter-productive.
- Describe this incident to them in clear, precise terms.
- Make a direct link between the behavior you describe and the fact that you are having this conversation with them.
- Outline the consequences you perceive they are creating for themselves by using this approach, such as damaging their reputation, excluding themselves from particular project work, or preventing themselves from being considered for work alongside more senior or influential managers.
- Should you want to make your feedback even stronger, you could also say that should they be unable to amend their conduct you will need to revisit the issues with them again.

These last point two points are crucial. You need to spell out the direct unpleasant consequences for your employee of their again behaving in an adversarial way towards you or the organization which employs them. Only you as their manager can decide what these consequences will be. It is the expectation that they will be in trouble if they don't amend their ways that will motivate most adversarial team members to use different behavior.

Some adversarial team members may not even realize how self-destructive they are being, and may need time to absorb your feedback before you move on to outline the consequences you will enforce should they fail to use a more productive approach in future. Others will be fully aware of the hot water they are in and that it is their approach that has turned up the heat. But whatever consequences you decide upon, you must be prepared to enforce them as soon as you observe your team member again using adversarial behavior. If you don't, they will learn that they can get away with it, and will continue to use counterproductive and self-destructive behavior.

YOUR ADVERSARIAL COLLEAGUES

You might like to apply the material from the second half of this chapter to your own team. Answer the following questions and jot down your response to each of them in the spaces below:

■ Identify a team member whom you think displays adversarial traits. What steps have you taken to confront their behavior?

■ What changes have you observed in their behavior as a result of using this approach?

■ What additional steps, if any, will you now take to encourage them towards a more productive way of doing things?

SUMMARY AND NEXT CHAPTER

This chapter concentrated on the issues surrounding having an adversarial member in your team. The chapter suggested that taking adversarial behavior at face value will result in your failing to address the real underlying motives of your team member, and won't get you very far. It highlighted how clever such a team member can be at obfuscating the issues when you do confront them. The chapter identified that team members who are antagonistic towards authority can be helped to amend their ways if they are handled in the right way. It presented several alternative ways of doing this, one based on generosity of spirit, the other based on effective feedback skills. The chapter demonstrated the pivotal role that you, the manager of an adversarial team member, have in shaping their future behavior by naming the game or by suggesting that you are prepared to take action that will have unpleasant consequences for them should they fail to amend their conduct.

The next chapter will focus on the skills and strategies you need to employ should you find yourself working for an adversarial manager. The chapter will highlight the pitfalls and misjudgments that non-adversarial employees can make when reporting to an adversarial manager, one who has an adversarial mindset and organizational authority, and who therefore needs to be handled wisely.

CHAPTER 7

Reporting to an Adversarial Manager

Handling a Boss with Organizational Authority and an Adversarial Mindset

In this chapter we will examine the dynamics of reporting to and working for an adversarial manager. The chapter will explore how to handle the issues you are likely to encounter as an employee reporting to an adversarial boss. It will highlight the pitfalls, mistakes, and misjudgments that you could make as you tackle the dual challenges of your manager's adversarial intent and their significant organizational authority. The chapter will examine the ins and outs of a situation in which your boss may try to use the power available to them in their role to intimidate or undermine you rather than support you, may be unusually confrontational and antagonistic towards you even when you are performing effectively and may deliberately play you off against members of your peer group or vice versa. It will explore the unique situation of finding that your manager chooses to behave in these ways on a repeat basis, regardless of how effectively you are performing, have performed or are likely to perform in the future.

The chapter will present the view that it will not be in your best interests to expend energy trying to:

- Change your adversarial manager into a non-adversarial manager – it won't work.
- Win their approval and positive regard – they aren't likely to let you build bridges with them or become warmer and more supportive towards you.
- Change your way of handling yourself at work wholesale to compensate for your manager's behavior – you don't need to.

Instead the chapter will propose that, just as with adversarial peers and adversarial team members, it is the quality of behavior you use in the adversarial moment that is important, and given the organizational authority available to your boss, it is vital you handle yourself well every time you meet them. The chapter illustrates a series of effective ways of handling an adversarial boss, and suggests that the best way to manage the situation will be to present yourself as a valued adviser to your manager despite the degree of difficulty their behavior will inevitably create for you. You can do this by:

- Concentrating on performing in your role as effectively as you can.
- Responding to your manager's requests and requirements of you promptly and fully.
- Respecting their position as your boss.
- Seeking to add value to their plans whenever you can by disagreeing carefully with them when you need to, suggesting alternative ways forward that they might want to consider, and giving them a heads up on issues which you think they may need to know about.

The chapter suggests that by respecting your manager's *office* and working diligently at your *role* you stand a good chance of steering a course between:

- Wasting energy worrying about what your manager *might* do next or *might* require of you that you won't like.
- Keeping your attention where it needs to be, on handling your duties effectively.
- Reacting to their adversarial behavior and losing your focus or confidence.
- Taking advantage of opportunities to demonstrate to your boss just how much value you add to the organization.

The chapter will begin by exploring the differences between an adversarial and a non-adversarial manager's use of the power available to them in their role. It will then examine some of the key characteristics of an adversarial manager's behavior before highlighting the impact that repeated exposure to these tactics can have on you, your workplace interests, and your well-being. We will then explore what behavior to use and what to avoid when dealing with an adversarial manager in the normal course of events, as well as how to disagree effectively with someone who will not automatically welcome your engaging with them in this way. We will examine how to handle a confrontation with an adversarial manager in a situation in which you cannot win, so that you make your points and lose less rather than make your points and lose entirely. We will then outline the benefits of keeping your eye on the role you are there to perform in all your dealings with your adversarial manager, rather than falling into the trap of either reacting to their adversarial tactics acting out of fear or out of an attempt to change them and win their approval. We will illustrate the principles presented in the chapter with some realistic examples, and also take a look at your own experiences of working with adversarial managers.

COMPARING AN ADVERSARIAL MANAGER AND A NON-ADVERSARIAL MANAGER

Adversarial managers use the power available to them in their roles differently from non-adversarial managers. Those of you with first-hand knowledge of the dynamics created by an adversarial manager will recognize this fact straightaway. Bearing in mind that each manager, whether adversarial or non-adversarial, is unique and has their own individual way of handling their workplace relationships and their organizational authority, let's begin by outlining some of the key features of a non-adversarial way of managing before moving on to consider the differences that an adversarial manager creates.

How a Non-adversarial Manager Uses Their Organizational Authority

Depending on how well you have developed your leadership, management, influencing, and people-handling skills those of you who see yourselves as non-adversarial managers are likely to regard your organizational authority as a tool through which to get things done. This tool may prove useful in regards to many aspects of your role including:

- Altering the values by which your part of the organization operates by, for instance, improving the customer focus of the organization or raising the standard of the coaching skills demonstrated by your managers.
- Changing your organization's goals so that, for instance, it adopts new and more incisive marketing strategies or higher financial targets.

- Setting more stretching development objectives for the individuals or teams who report to you.
- Securing additional budget to spend on improved equipment or engaging the services of more able, better qualified, and more experienced employees.
- Finding out what improvements your customers want to see the organization deliver before implementing suitable changes to bring about those outcomes.

Those of you who identify with a non-adversarial style of management may regard having organizational power as something of a bonus, a bonus which enables you to play a deeper role in setting the agenda for your part of the organization and one that means that you can get certain things done quicker and more effectively than if you don't have a degree of organizational authority. However, you may also regard having a degree of organizational authority as a double-edged sword. It enables you to get things done and is therefore useful, but it also carries significant responsibility with it, responsibility that, depending on how conscientious you are, can weigh heavily on your shoulders.

Having organizational authority means that your opinion carries more weight than the opinion of someone with less organizational status, so you need to have something valuable and relevant to contribute at every meeting in which you participate. Having organizational authority means that your attitude and conduct affect your team members' behavior, and some of them may actually mirror them. It means that your staff will be influenced by your values, so you need to make sure that at all times you role model the workplace principles, standards and ethics that you want your employees to adopt. Having organizational authority also means that, even though you have the greater influence, some of your staff will know more about certain issues than you do, so you need to find effective ways of working with them without either failing to elicit their knowledge for fear of looking out of touch or accessing it in a way that demeans your own status. Having organizational authority means that your team members will be on the lookout for signals to help them discern:

- Your attitude to them.
- The degree to which you respect them.
- The extent to which you place your confidence in them.
- The level at which you approve of their work.

- What you don't like about them and what they do for you.
- Situations in which you don't rate them or their input.
- Whether or not you think that they add sufficient value to your organization.

Your instinct as a non-adversarial manager will be, to whatever extent, to work hard at leading and managing your team to create a working culture that supports effective performance and serves customers well. Overall, as a non-adversarial manager, you are likely to have dual concerns, concerns that are to:

- Utilize the power available to you in your role to improve your organization whenever and wherever your can.
- Build productive workplace relationships with your team members, supporting them to achieve their goals, giving them room within which to perform effectively, providing them with clear feedback when they don't perform well, and rewarding them fairly for a job well done.

How an Adversarial Manager Uses Their Organizational Authority

However, those of you who work for an adversarial manager will not recognize much of the above description. While an adversarial manager may have a similar job description to a non-adversarial manager, they also have a totally different attitude to both their team members and to the power available to them in their role. An adversarial manager will still demand success from each and every member of their workforce. But the instincts that drive them are completely different from those of their non-adversarial colleagues, and therefore the methods they use to manage and lead are quite different too. These methods can involve a greater emphasis on intimidation and on demonstrations of raw power than would normally be the case, and can also involve extending far lower levels of trust and support to you and their other team members than you might need or want.

An adversarial manager will expect you and the other employees working for them to do what you need to do to succeed in your role, whether or not you find their style, methods or values helpful or conducive. They may simply not care that their approach renders you less effective at certain aspects of your job than a less adversarial approach would do. They may be uninterested in the fact that their style of managing you doesn't sit comfortably with you or accord with the kind of input you want from a manager. They may not be willing to receive any feedback on these issues, may not value the feedback you do give, or may simply be indifferent to your opinion of them. Worse still, by virtue of the fact that an adversarial manager plays a managerial role, they may well have the active support of their own manager who might not recognize your description of them should you choose to relate it to them.

Working for an adversarial manager is unlikely to involve you in a participative or collaborative process. Rather than 'My door is always open' it is more likely to be a matter of 'My door is always open but be careful when you come in.'

Working for a non-adversarial manager is likely to be a two-way street in which you and your manager work to achieve goals of relevance to your employer, albeit that you have differing job descriptions and differing degrees of organizational power. But working for an adversarial manager is likely to be a one-way street in which your manager regards their job as being to prod, push, cajole, challenge, command, intimidate, and if necessary threaten you and their other team members towards achieving your goals. They could well regard their organizational power as an extension of themselves, a tool which they can utilize whenever they feel the need to. And the range of circumstances in which an adversarial manager can feel moved to use threats, coercion, and raw power to get things done, as opposed to demonstrating a range of people-handling and influencing skills, can be extensive.

An adversarial manager is likely to relate to their own wishes and their own opinion in an idiosyncratic way. They will often expect that their requirements, or to put it another way their *will*, should take precedence over the wishes of anyone else involved in a particular scenario, even scenarios in which theirs might not be the most informed view. While many non-adversarial managers are often disposed to debate and discuss issues, are open to being influenced over certain considerations, and are ready to negotiate on others, an adversarial manager may not be prepared to do some or any of these things. Sometimes, they could offer a view or give an opinion in a situation that it is your or another team member's responsibility to handle, and which you or your team colleague rightly thinks sits with you. At these times, it can be unclear to you whether you have received an order, a suggestion, or simply an expression of interest.

The Impact of Adversarial Managers

Working for an adversarial manager is a difficult thing to do. It can be a very taxing indeed. For one thing, it will take considerable objectivity on your part to consistently remind yourself that your boss's tactics are not aimed at you personally. *He or she is like that*, and he or she is like that with everyone. They are busy handling their relationships in an adversarial way because that is what they do, and it's the strategy they are using at that time, in that place. At some level your adversarial manager may well understand that their approach is unreasonable and difficult for their staff to deal with. But they probably don't care very much about that. It is an approach they are taking because it serves their purpose and they take it consistently.

Working for an adversarial manager can also feel like a risky thing to do. Those of you who find yourselves in this position may consider that your role involves you in carrying a constant level of personal risk that your performance doesn't warrant. The dual fears that lurk in your mind are likely to be:

- Under what circumstances will you need to leave your employment to maintain your integrity?
- Under what circumstances will your boss's methods result in you failing at or losing your job?

You may feel a degree of powerlessness at the unhappy situation you find yourself in. Your boss's approach might actually make it more difficult for you to get done the things you need to get done, and you may have limited options available to you for addressing this situation. You could:

- Give your manager feedback on the adverse impact of their conduct on you, but you may well find that they are not interested in the feedback, don't change anything as a result of hearing it, or worse still, escalate their adversarial tactics thereafter.
- Refer the matter to your boss's boss, but having hierarchical authority over your boss, they may well not encounter the adversarial tactics you run into, and even if they respect the fact that they exist, may not want to address them. You also run the risk of alienating your own manager still further by going over their head.
- Discuss the issues with your peers and allies to see how they respond to your feedback on your boss's style, a strategy which

may well prove reassuring if they also regard your manager as adversarial, but a strategy which won't actually change any of the dynamics in your relationship with your boss.

■ Continue to carry out your work as best you can, but do so with less and less enthusiasm, passion, or resolve.

■ Mentally resign and do just enough to get by in your role.

■ Seek a move to another part of the organization or to another employer.

However, it is important to bear in mind that your manager does need someone to carry out the role you perform, and replacing you will take time. And you do have some options for handling their behavior as and when it happens, options that the chapter will outline in due course.

Lower Levels of Trust and Support

One factor that is particularly unsettling for those of you who report to a truly adversarial manager is that your manager will find it difficult to extend usual levels of trust or support towards you even when you have repeatedly demonstrated competence in your key performance indicators. Their preference will be for putting you and their other team members under continual pressure, requiring you to justify your outputs even when there hasn't been any indication that your performance standards have slipped. Some adversarial managers are relentless at adopting this approach. They will be unwilling to act supportively towards you and their other team members even when it would be helpful for them to do so given their workplace goals. Instead, they will prefer to keep themselves detached and separate from you and their other team members' concerns, neither apparently interested nor uninterested in the details of any evolving situation, but watchful and aware nonetheless. Then they will suddenly engage with a scenario, which, until their unexpected input, they appeared to be disengaged from. A truly adversarial manager will prefer to remain distant from and unrelaxed towards you and their other employees at all times, keeping a skeptical eye out for signs of error, omission, or incompetence even in consistently effective performers. They may even engage with you in such a way that each time you meet them it feels as if it's the first time you are doing so.

Working for an adversarial manager will involve you in constant challenges to prove yourself often without corresponding messages of praise when you do succeed. Many adversarial managers eschew failure to such an extent that they expect success, require it, even demand it but then don't react with pleasure when it occurs. Rather, unable to enjoy the moment, they accept the outcome as a done deal and move on immediately to look for another target to set for you, their other staff and their organization, often without pausing to celebrate or even note the positive result. They can quickly find themselves out of step with their staff but are likely to be unconcerned that this is the case.

Working for an adversarial manager will involve you in managing a relationship that adds to the degree of unhelpful challenge you face at work. For those of you who would prefer to work for a manager whose wisdom, contacts and support provide a useful source of reference for you in your work, this can be a taxing situation to find yourself in. The conduct of a truly adversarial manager will create tension in their relationship with you, through both what they don't do – such as offer you active support or respond to your requests for input – and the ways in which they do behave, such as undermining you or acting on the erroneous presupposition that you are in danger of failing unless they see to it that you don't.

So, given all the challenges inherent in handling an adversarial manager what behavior will serve you well and what behavior will work against you when you are in a meeting with your boss? Consider the following example, which is set in a drug manufacturer.

CASE STUDY 16: MANAGING THE MANAGER

The manager of research and development in a pharmaceutical manufacturer is an adversarial manager. Her style is unusually combative, and she routinely puts her team members under pressure. She calls one of her team members into her office and tells him to sit. Then she tells him that she wants to speak with him about his team's current development project, to identify what he could be doing differently and better. There are a number of ways in which the team member could respond to this opening. Let's examine three of them.

■ The team member hears this opening as an undermining one and feels defensive. In the split second it takes him to process her words, a number of worries go through his mind. He worries that his manager knows something he doesn't that affects the status of the project. He worries that he or one of his staff has put a foot wrong and it has come to the attention of his boss before him. He worries that what he says next will have great bearing on a decision that his manager is mulling over, the purpose and details of which are unknown to him but which involves him, and he worries that he is now in a trap because he doesn't know the situation he is about to address. During the instant that these worries pass through his mind the team member feels paralyzed. Then he pulls himself together and starts to outline where he has got to with the project.

■ The team member hears this opening as a challenge and feels energized. He tells his manager that he has been giving this question some thought and is calling a team meeting for the following afternoon to address the issue. He then asks his manager whether or not she would like to attend.

■ The team member hears this opening as an indication that his manager has something she wants to say. He asks her what is on her mind.

Managing the Manager: Analyzing the Dynamics

Let's revisit this situation to analyze the dynamics in it. In this example an adversarial manager calls one of her team members into her office and tells him to sit down. The absence of pleasantries such as 'hello' or 'how is your day going?' coupled with the command to sit creates an adversarial atmosphere straight away, and the team member is on high alert from the off. His boss then says that she wants to speak with him about his team's current development project, to identify what he could be doing differently and better. Depending on how he hears this ambivalent opening, he could play the meeting effectively or mess it up. Let's see how he gets on.

■ In the first instance, the team member hears this opening as an undermining slight. He takes it as a statement that implies that he isn't doing that good a job at managing the project and needs to find some improvement opportunities quickly. Having heard her calculatedly ambiguous words as a slur on his handling of his responsibilities, he immediately starts to worry. A series of self-defeating anxieties run through his mind, each of which rapidly succeeds the previous one. In the split second it takes him to generate three potential causes of concern he becomes paralyzed with anxiety. His worst fear is that his manager is handling a decision unknown to him but involving him and will place undue weight on whatever he says next. He worries that, should he mishandle the moment, he will seal his own fate. However, he quickly gets a grip on his fear and starts to outline where he has got to with the project. Sadly for him, his factual analysis of the status quo of the project doesn't do it. It may be safe territory – he does know his stuff – but it doesn't address the issue that his boss put to him. That issue is what he and his team could be doing differently and better in their management of the project. She doesn't want a status update. He has gone off down the wrong tack, and will quickly find that his irritable and impatient manager pulls him back. This is not a good start, and his poor performance at the beginning of the meeting could result in the rest of it being unnecessarily difficult for him to deal with.

■ In the second instance, the team member hears his boss's opening gambit as a challenge to which he instantly rises. He is afraid of her and doesn't want to give her any reason to think that he is not on top of his game. However, his response to her opening involves a lie. He makes something up straight away, which is a risky thing to do and might backfire on him in due course. He says, quite dishonestly, that he has already thought about the issue of what to improve and how on the project. He says that he is in the process of calling a team meeting to address this issue on the following day, and invites his manager to attend it. None of this is true, and his manager might subsequently find that out, and be displeased to say the least. However, his invitation is an effective way of throwing her off guard. It buys him time and lets him out of a tight corner, although only time will tell how useful a gambit it proves to be in the long run. His boss draws the meeting to a close quite quickly when she says she will check her diary for the following afternoon and get back to him. By demonstrating a high degree of openness to her despite her adversarial nature, he creates the impression that he has nothing to hide from her and is confident about the quality of the meeting that he says he is arranging. She may or may not want to attend the meeting, but she will likely be satisfied that this team member has responded effectively to her enquiry. However, he will have to go ahead and set up the meeting whether or not she wants to attend it, and hope that she doesn't find out that he only thought to call it after he met with her. He will also have to provide his manager with a full and effective set of suggestions for upgrading the project following the meeting.

■ In the third instance, the team member decides that his boss has a specific reason for posing her question, and asks her what is on her mind. He is not defensive, scared, or threatened by her enquiry, but instead sees the question as an opportunity to build credibility with her. By switching the focus of the meeting away from him and back to her in this respectful and low-key way he demonstrates that he on the lookout for ways to add value to her agenda. He tells her that he is listening for what she wants to achieve, and is prepared to consider and work with her agenda. He sidesteps all the pitfalls he would fall into should he interpret her question as a challenge to him or as an insult about his management of his project, or should he be tempted to lie to her out of fear. And he demonstrates to her that self-doubt is not at the top of his list of attributes. She may have something on her mind or she may not. But she will learn that this particular team member is not easily shaken, is confident in his role, and focused on working well with her.

In this example we see how your initial response to an adversarial manager's enquiry makes all the difference to how the meeting progresses and what impression you make in the mind of your manager.

YOUR ADVERSARIAL COLLEAGUES

You might like to spend a few minutes considering your own experiences of working for an adversarial manager. You can jot down your answers to the following questions in the spaces below:

■ Identify a manager for whom you have worked whom you consider to be adversarial. What does this manager do or say that leads you to believe that they have adversarial traits?

■ What impact does this manager's adversarial approach create for you in your work?

■ What methods of handling them have you employed?

■ In what ways have these methods proved effective in helping you manage your relationship with this manager? In what ways have they been ineffective?

■ Identify a specific meeting in which your adversarial manager put you on the back foot from the start. Looking back on it now, how could you have handled the start of the meeting so that you remained on the front foot?

THE AIM OF AN ADVERSARIAL MANAGER

Adversarial managers act in the ways described above so that they can test the mettle of their team members. They use this approach because they want to know how robust you are and how effectively you will stand up to them. Many adversarial managers test their staff on a continual basis because they want to evaluate how:

■ Well defended you are.
■ Self-confident and self-starting you are.
■ Well equipped you are to handle your workplace affairs autonomously and independently.
■ Far you will go to protect your interests at work.
■ Effective you might be at using self-respecting and self-preserving behavior under pressure.

They want to know to what extent you are equipped to:

■ Stand up to them respectfully.
■ Remain resolute when under pressure to justify yourself and your approach to your work.
■ Respect your own judgments, opinions, and points of view, and remain committed to them under fire.
■ Handle them in consistently effective ways.

The criteria that an adversarial manager uses to assess whom among their team members they rate and whom they do not rate may be, from your point of view, quite limited. And even if they rate you, they are unlikely to show it by communicating a degree of liking and respect for you or your work. It is likely that one of the key criteria that an adversarial manager employs in forming an assessment of any team member is the extent to which any individual employee is willing to give an alternative view to theirs, because *it is what they actually think* rather than because it is:

■ What they think their adversarial manager wants to hear.
■ A reflection of their fear of the adversarial manager or the degree of intimidation they feel in their presence.
■ A view they have generated in reaction to their manager's point of view simply because they don't like their manager's style, feel angry with them, and want to contest the point with them.
■ Something to say, because it's better to say something which you have not thought through properly or to which you have no commitment than to say nothing at all.

THE CHALLENGE OF WORKING FOR AN ADVERSARIAL MANAGER

Working for an adversarial manager is a supreme test of a team member's maturity and resolve. It is difficult to work for someone who never seems satisfied with your performance no matter how good it is. It is difficult to work for someone who might occasionally say 'good job' but who generally doesn't, and who, even when they do, can immediately devalue the praise with some remark about what could have been done better or differently. It is difficult to work for someone who:

■ Doesn't respect the boundaries around your work.
■ Doesn't support you.

■ Actively mistrusts you or remains aloof and detached from you.
■ Tactically introduces dynamics into their relationship with you that are designed to keep you on your toes, to demonstrate their power over you, to remind you of who is in charge, and to test your resolve as and when they feel the need.

Depending on your constitution and what it is you need from a manager, these dynamics can leave you feeling vulnerable, tired, confused, demoralized, or all of these. Consider the following example.

CASE STUDY 17: STRAIGHT ANSWER TO A STRAIGHT QUESTION

The owner of a small but successful retail chain is an adversarial manager. She approaches each of the eight management team members who report to her at head office with a mixture of mistrust, antagonism, and expectation. Albeit unconsciously, she expects them all to fail if she doesn't keep on top of them, and she consequently sees her job as being to challenge them and, as she sees it, motivate them towards more effective performance. She has a particular fear of her staff members becoming complacent in their work, and this fear kicks in after each and every one of their successes.

At these times she approaches each member of the management team with either a sharp complaint about their conduct or a remark about their performance on a particular piece of recent work. She prefers to make these comments publicly, often also suggesting that a particular management team member's success was partly down to luck or good fortune rather than wholly down to application and skill. Over the years that she has owned her business she has lost a steady trickle of head office staff, each of whom has been asked to leave or has grown weary of the atmosphere her behavior creates in the head office. However, she never has any difficulty finding replacements. Her hires are a mixture of people who don't have a high need for connection at work and people who do. Several members of the current management team are relieved that their work takes them out of the office from time to time so that they can get away from the atmosphere that their boss creates.

The more autonomous members of her management team are sufficiently irked by her way of handling them that they try to improve her opinion of them. Determined to prove her wrong, they take her rebukes on the chin, work harder, and challenge themselves afresh in the hope of altering her perception and securing her good opinion. Having received ambivalent feedback or miserly praise, they don't give in but resist her characterizations of them and redouble their efforts straightaway. The other members of the management team, while initially keen to secure their boss's good opinion of them, take a different tack. When another good performance is overlooked this group of team members begin to realize that their boss might not have that much approval to give them however well they perform. They think that the way their manager carries on in the office demotivates them and is wholly counterproductive. This group of peers start to let her verbal barbs go over their heads, effectively ignoring them and her. Until, that is, she decides to open a new store and lets it be known that she will ask one of the management team to run it for her. Then she starts to play one member of the management team off against another.

On a Monday morning the adversarial manager observes one of her management team members arriving early for work, and follows her to her office. She has ambivalent feelings about this member of the team, simultaneously regarding her as someone who could give more to the company, and as someone whom she thinks would rather work somewhere else. The business owner walks into her team member's office and tells her that she wants a straight answer to a straight question. After the briefest of pauses, during which time her team member barely has time to collect her thoughts, the adversarial manager demands to know whether or not this employee thinks that the management team peer with whom she has been working recently is up to the job of managing the new store single-handedly.

Straight Answer to a Straight Question: Analyzing the Dynamics

Let's revisit this scenario to analyze its dynamics and explore the ins and outs of the situation. In this scenario the owner of a small but successful chain of retail outlets is also the manager of a team of eight people in the company's head office. She is an adversarial manager, one who uses her power to threaten, cajole, and antagonize her staff into performing more effectively, a strategy she employs out of a deep-seated fear that without her best attentions her management team will coast and not perform effectively. so letting her down and leaving the company she has built in a parlous state.

The adversarial manager doesn't see the inconsistency in her thinking: that she has hired and paid each and every one of these employees presumably because she did not think they would fail and did think they were qualified for the role for which she hired them. Instead, she continues to employ them while actively mistrusting them to differing degrees and failing to offer usual levels of support to any of them. Neither does she alter her point of view and reassess her deep-seated fear after working with a particular team member for a number of weeks or months. She maintains her steadfast conviction that all of her management team members could potentially fail her if she doesn't see to it that they don't. The business owner is assiduous in looking for opportunities to keep her staff on their toes, even jumping on them when they are enjoying the immediate upshot of a workplace success. She is so afraid of failure that it colors her view of all her staff all the time, no matter what the particular circumstances in the business.

However, some of the members of her management team do respond well to her style. They regard her challenging methods as well-intentioned attempts to keep standards high in an ever more competitive marketplace. Being natural self-starters, these members of the workforce redouble their efforts, set higher standards for themselves, and set about proving to their manager that her assessment of them is wrong. Other members of staff do not share this view. They grow tired of the same adversarial tactics being used by their manager, who they come to see as limited in her ability to manage people. This group of employees think that the impulse behind her approach is not an objective assessment of them or their capabilities. They think that she has no genuine reason to doubt them. They regard her reservations about them as a symptom of a doubt that is internal to her, that *she puts onto them* regardless of how well they have performed or are performing. It is this dynamic that creates cynicism in them, and which results in them feeling demotivated by her tactics. Nonetheless, she is their boss and their employer, so while they do not like her approach to managing them and they continue to regard it as counterproductive in the long term, they don't let her know how unhelpful they find it. The eight members of the management team are all hard working and continue to do their best, albeit with relief that their roles take them away from the office for a few days at a time every now and then.

However, the dynamic in the office changes when the business owner alters tack and starts to play one team member off against another. This change of tactic coincides with her decision to open a new store and her subsequent need to appoint a full-time store manager from amongst the management team members. She selects a team member who she believes is holding back and about whom she harbors some misgivings. While never quite able to put her finger on what it is about this employee that results in her harboring such a high degree of doubt about her, the business owner nonetheless thinks that she doesn't really want to work for the company. She selects her as the target for her change of tactics and chooses her moment carefully. On a Monday morning when this management team member has made a special effort to get in early, the business owner follows her to her office. She doesn't say 'good morning' or ask her employee about her weekend. Instead she comes right out with it without preamble, and says that she wants a straight answer to a straight question. She leaves a minute pause, one insufficiently long to give her team member time to get her bearings or to ask what the context for the meeting is. Then the business owner asks her whether or not she thinks that one of her peers, a peer with whom she has been working closely for some time and with whom she has established liking and rapport, will be able to handle managing the new outlet single-handedly.

The management team member is in a tricky position. She is well aware of the adversarial nature of her employer. She has heard her make antagonistic comments around the office. She has been on the receiving end of her barbed critiques in the past. But this is a new tactic, and one that throws her. Her boss is asking her for an opinion on one of her colleagues, a colleague with whom she has been working closely, but a colleague whom she is now being asked to comment on behind his back. She wants to be considered for the new store manager role herself, and she knows full well that her boss wouldn't hesitate to pass her over for the role should she appear uncertain, unsure, or reluctant to give an answer. And this despite the fact that she is well qualified in her terms of experience and skill to handle the role effectively.

If the management team member remains loyal to her colleague and says 'Yes, he can handle the new role single-handedly,' her boss may interpret this as her deliberately passing up the opportunity to manage the new store herself. This would go down very badly with a manager who expects constant energy, enthusiasm, and proactive conduct from her management team members. If the management team member puts herself first and says, 'No, he cannot handle the new role single-handedly,' she will feel that she has let down a colleague she likes and works well with, and whom she actually thinks would do a good job as a store manager. If she ducks the question, passing it back to her boss with the words 'You need to decide for yourself,' she risks appearing weak and vacillating, a combination her boss despises. In a split second she must decide how to play this awkward situation and how to respond to an enquiry which represents anything but a request for a straight answer to a straight question. We will return to this situation later on in the chapter to see how the management team member handles it.

THE MINDSET OF AN ADVERSARIAL MANAGER

We have been exploring an example in which an adversarial manager feels the need to play one employee off against another. This is a deliberate act on her part, one designed to create tension between the two colleagues even though only one of them is in the room at the time she sets up the dynamic between them. Her maneuver enables her to set the two of them up to vie against one another. It enables her to observe:

- What the team member she confronts is made of.
- How this team member will handle the invitation to do down her colleague.
- To what extent this team member will maintain her integrity when placed under this much pressure.

The adversarial manager will gain a lot of information about her employee from handling things in this way. She will be unconcerned at the impact of her tactic on the working relationship between her two team members. In fact it will serve her purpose as she tries to divide two people who have worked well together. She believes that by creating tension between them she will motivate both colleagues to try to outperform the other. She is a complicated character, at once motivated by a need to achieve and to see her staff achieve, but also equally motivated by the fear that they might not, and that their possible failure will pollute her and injure her company. This dual tension between a personal fear of failure and the consequent need to achieve, and the fear that those around her will fail her if she doesn't prevent them from doing so, drives many of her actions at work. What other conclusions can we draw about the mindset of this adversarial manager?

She does not value affiliation, trust, or support at work. Not only does she not value these things in her own working life, she despises these needs in others. She does not recognize the need for these kinds of workplace bonds, and views them as illegitimate and risible. She acts to destroy these connections between colleagues just as much as she acts to preclude them developing in her own working relationships. She doesn't see the need for harmony, liking, consensus, or enjoyment in the workplace. She prefers to keep her workplace relationships cool and distant, or at least uninvolved, as this enables her to make clean business decisions uncontaminated by the unwelcome distractions of people-oriented considerations like loyalty or compassion. Instead, she values independence and autonomy to a huge extent, both in herself and in the people she employs. She is a fiercely independent person, prone to keeping an unusual degree of emotional distance between herself and her employees. She wants to be able to operate, as she sees it, effectively while keeping a considerable degree of distance between herself and her colleagues, and she would like to see her employees doing the same thing too. In fact, she admires employees who are able to thrive in the kinds of environments she creates, those marked by constant friction and enmity, low levels of trust, and low levels of support. She believes that employees who can operate autonomously in this kind of environment make for better employees than those who produce their best work in tandem with collegial others.

What else can we say about her? We can say that she doesn't readily make the link between her team members consistently producing effective outputs and her team members having developed high-quality relationships with one another. Not needing affiliations at work herself, she denies her staff the very real connections which some of them need to perform well, and instead either makes continuous, destabilizing changes to the team, placing unnecessary pressure on her team members, or surrounds herself with people whose mindset is similar to hers and who also have a low need for trusting, supportive connections at work. Those team members who want to work in a close-knit team and who enjoy some degree of trusting, supportive contact with their colleagues are unlikely to choose to remain working for her for long if there is an alternative option available to them.

Also, this adversarial manager is not a good listener. She gives undue weight to her own internally generated view of a situation or an employee, a view that can be formed without reference to other potentially useful sources of information, and on the basis of a series of assumptions that she does not take the time to reality test. Having formed a view, she can be quite wedded to it and difficult to shift from it. Not only might she react adversely to an attempt to do so, but also

assigned by the senior partner sits at the top. He doesn't like being told to reorder his work schedule, and replies aggressively. He tells his boss that he is engaged on a number of projects that earn money for the firm, and doesn't want to jeopardize the standard of the work he is doing by moving his attention elsewhere to an internally focused project.

■ The divisional director shifts slightly in his seat. He ignores the question and returns to his previous point. He tells his boss politely but firmly that any review of performance assessment methods ought to include input from human resources. He suggests that he manages the project and reports to the senior partner on its progress, but that he also includes someone from HR in the work so that he can make use of their expertise. He ends by saying that, as it appears that the senior partner wants to see progress being made on the project quite quickly, it would speed things up if he could work with one of the HR colleagues he already knows. He says that he will formulate a project plan including timescales and come back to his boss by the end of the day.

Creating a Senior Enemy: Analyzing the Dynamics

Let's revisit this situation to analyze the dynamics in it. We will explore the motivation of the new senior partner and the impact on him of the different ways in which the divisional director handles him.

In this example a newly appointed adversarial senior partner meets all of his divisional heads one-to-one before selecting one particular person to whom to assign to a new project. The divisional director he selects has no experience relevant to carrying out the new performance management project. The senior partner is quite deliberate in his choice, selecting a divisional director who is already fully committed with client-facing work and who, while undertaking the project, will be well outside his comfort zone. The senior partner wishes to place him in this position because he wants to see how he reacts and what he can learn about his character. The senior partner sits the divisional director down and, rather like a schoolmaster, asks him to outline his current list of priorities. The divisional director takes a breath and starts to do so. He is used to giving sharp summaries in the course of his day-to-day work and this skill comes in handy in this meeting. However, he is part way through a précis of his second project when his new boss interrupts him to inform him that he has something else for him to do.

The senior partner then outlines what this additional task consists of, and the divisional director is surprised that it involves him in a project outside of his area of expertise. In fact, it is a project that focuses on the way in which the firm handles its assessment and reward of effective performance. The divisional director suggests, reasonably enough, that he works alongside a colleague from human resources on the project, and is again surprised when his new boss shakes his head and reiterates that he wants the divisional director to undertake the work. He doesn't say that he wants the divisional director to work single-handedly on the project, but that seems to be the implication. Respectful towards authority, the divisional director says he will add the project to his work list, and mentally prepares to leave the meeting. The divisional director is not an expert in performance management, and he lacks the ability to carry out the project effectively on his own. He hopes that this maneuver will buy him time so that he can either research the issues or influence his boss to change his mind about the involvement of someone from HR. However, he is pulled up short when his boss asks the pointed question 'How long is the list?' The implication is that the adversarial manager wants this new assignment to take precedence over the divisional director's other work so that he can start it immediately. The Divisional Director's attempt to buy time has backfired. He cannot avoid dealing with his situation here and now. Let's see how the divisional director responds to this challenge.

■ In the first instance, the divisional director feels angry with his boss for apparently setting him up to fail, and lets it show. He considers that he is the wrong person to carry out this project, and objects to the fact that his boss is browbeating him into taking on a piece of work he knows he won't perform well on. He quickly moves into a mode in which he is motivated solely by his own ire and his opposition to his manager. He forms the view that his new boss is misusing his authority, and decides that he must prevent him from introducing this, as he sees it, destructive dynamic into his relationship with him. So he goes onto the offensive straightaway and puts forward a strongly worded counter-argument. He tells his boss that in other circumstances he would be quite willing to carry out the project but that he cannot do so straightaway because of his client commitments. He tells his boss that it would be better to assign the project to someone who is immediately available to start it. Then he has a direct go at him. He informs his boss that it would be better to place the project in the hands of someone who has the relevant expertise and skills to handle the project effectively. His choice of words is poor, even if his sentiment is understandable. He questions his boss's judgment and suggests that he is making a mistake in assigning the project to him. This is a highly antagonistic way of handling the encounter with his boss. In his own mind, the divisional director thinks that he needs to make a robust counter to his boss's proposal, but in reality his hostility leaves him with little room for maneuver. He may well feel justified in expressing his anger at his new boss's tactics and, as he sees it, in robustly defending his right to decide what work he accepts and what works he leaves for someone better placed to handle it. But he has done so in a way that will antagonize his boss, who will regard his conduct as disrespectful to his authority. And he will look for another opportunity to reinforce the message that he is in charge and demands to be respected. The divisional director may have stood up for himself, but he has also created a set of circumstances that may well rebound badly on him in due course.

■ In the second instance, the divisional director reacts to his boss's attempt, as he sees it, to reprioritize his work for him. He doesn't want to jeopardize his current client-facing commitments, and doesn't want to be told how to handle his workload by his new boss. He decides to push back, and uses an argument that he thinks will appeal to the businessman in his boss. He tells him that he is actively engaged in working with clients and earning income for the firm. He says that he does not want to jeopardize the standard of work he is doing for his clients by moving his eye from those projects to an internally focused one. But his strategy is not well thought out. The senior partner is well aware of the client work being done by the divisional director and has factored it into his thinking. He has made clear his intention to assign him to the other project anyway. Worse still, the divisional director suggests that the senior partner is cavalier about client-facing work, and also intimates that he thinks that the new internally focused project devised by the senior partner is not as important as fee-earning work. These are not sound arguments to make to an adversarial manager, even if the divisional director does have a point. By locking horns with his boss and trying to point out the flaws in his thinking, the divisional director doesn't do himself any favors at all. Given their relative seniorities he can fully expect his boss to respond aggressively to what he will see as a misguided attempt to dissuade him from a course of action to which he is quite wedded.

In a way, it is the divisional director who has backed himself into a corner by his ill-judged response to his boss's pressurizing tactics.

■   In the third instance, the divisional director is quite clever. He ignores the senior partner's pointed question 'How long is the list?' and sidesteps it completely. Instead he addresses his boss's underlying concern that the new project be started sooner rather than later. He does so in a smooth and non-confrontational way. He suggests that he manage the project and report directly on its progress to the senior partner. Then he reiterates his view that the project needs HR input, but presents this way of handling things as a service to his boss. Recognizing that his boss would like the project to begin straightaway, the divisional director tells him that it would speed things up if he worked alongside an HR specialist he is familiar with. This makes it look as if his reasons for wanting to work with a colleague he knows from HR are to facilitate getting the project off the ground quickly and thereby better serve his manager. Actually, he would rather involve someone he knows from HR because he cannot accomplish the project without their input, and because he would prefer to work with someone he likes. This subtle but important shift in emphasis is important, and makes it more likely that the adversarial manager will agree to his proposal to work with someone from HR, even though he has already ruled it out. He will believe that the suggestion is being made with his needs in mind rather than the divisional director's, and will be impressed that the divisional director is prepared to reintroduce the idea into the conversation even though he has already rebuffed it. It is the style with which he does these things that wins the day for the divisional director. He maintains a non-confrontational, respectful, but assertive demeanor, avoids getting into a contest with his manager, and very clearly sticks to his guns. He then seizes the moment and takes control of the meeting. He says that he will devise a project plan by the end of the day and present it to his boss. Again, his boss will hear this as evidence of a proactive member of staff keen to meet his requirements of them. It is likely that his boss will agree to this way of handling things. He will have learnt that this divisional director is prepared to work with him, deliver to his wishes, and take on board his requirements. But he will also have learnt that he is quite capable of standing his ground, respecting his own point of view, remaining committed to that view under pressure, and effective at using the little room for maneuver available to him well. The divisional director's calculated gamble is one that presents his boss with a choice which he probably likes: respect my way of working, and I will respect yours *and* deliver to your requirements.

MAKING YOUR POINTS AND LOSING LESS

We have spent some time analyzing an example in which an adversarial manager asks one of his divisional directors to undertake a project which he is not well equipped to handle during a time when he is already fully occupied with client work. The divisional director has to find a way to handle the situation so that it doesn't look as if he is dodging the project, alienating his manager, antagonizing him, or failing to preserve his right to decide how he handles his workload and manages his responsibilities. Only in the third instance does the divisional director strike a sound balance between:

- Handling his boss's antagonistic manner.
- Taking the new project on board.
- Exercising choice about how to implement it.

While he still has to manage a project for which he does not have much relevant experience, and this may represent a loss of sorts to him, he has secured the right to work with an HR colleague familiar to him, and he has avoided the damaging defeat which would likely to come to him had he handled the meeting in a more oppositional or confrontational way, had he declined the project, or had he accepted it without HR involvement.

Finding a way to lose less can be an effective way of handling an adversarial manager. In some of the situations which your adversarial manager sets up there will be no way for you to engage them in a problem-solving, negotiating, or influencing conversation. Your manager may want you to do something, and you have to decide whether you will or you won't. If you really don't want to, and it is a matter of integrity for you, then you must do what your conscience dictates. But if you can see yourself going down the route that your adversarial manager wants you to adopt, even though you don't at first like the sound of it and might not even think you should be doing it, you may find that you lose less in the long run than if you antagonize your boss by trying to exert your will over theirs or bargain with them.

Questions to ask yourself at these times include:

- If I cooperate with my adversarial manager, what will I lose that I value?
- If I handle things the way my adversarial manager wants, what will I lose that I need?
- If I can see my way clear to taking on board my adversarial manager's wishes, what do I stand to gain that might be useful to me in the future?

MITIGATING THE RISKS OF COMPLIANCE

Those of you who recognize the challenge of having to handle tactics aimed at daunting you may be tempted from time to time to simply give in and comply with the wishes of your adversarial manager. The constant need to keep your boundaries in place and handle provoking behavior can prove wearing, and sometimes compliance appears to be quite an appealing option. However, compliance can carry a hidden cost and can actually prove to be quite an unwise thing to do. Consider the following short examples:

- An adversarial manager tells one of her team members to find out how many days off sick a particular team member has had in the past six months. The first team member is suspicious of her boss's motives in asking for this data, and is concerned that she may use the information against her colleague at some point in the future. But, unwilling to resist her antagonistic boss, she complies anyway and produces the data. Her boss learns that she can ask this team member to carry out tasks that involve her going behind a colleague's back, and that whether or not she has qualms about the work, she will carry it out. She starts to consider what other tasks she could line up for her to do.
- An adversarial manager asks two team members to carry out the same project. Up until that point both of the peers have been allies, and both of them have used supportive behavior with one another. When they are asked to carry out the same duties in direct competition with one another, one of the peers complies; the other objects. The compliant peer hopes that by giving his boss what he asks for, he will earn his favorable opinion. Sadly for him, his adversarial manager merely learns that he will acquiesce to his wishes to avoid a confrontation with him. He also learns that this peer places his wish for his manager's good opinion above other workplace considerations, including the quality of his working

relationship with his peer. The adversarial manager doesn't like what he regards as a weakness in this team member, and his disrespect for him grows even though he has done what he asked him to do.

In each of these situations the adversarial manager is testing the boundaries with one or more of their team members. In each case, the team member whose resolve is being tested lets the moment pass unopposed and complies with the wishes of their manager, even though in the first instance she experiences misgivings at taking the course of action requested of her. However, each of the main characters regrets their decision to comply with their manager's wishes when, farther down the line, it results in unpleasant consequences for them. Rather than win them a reprieve from further adversarial behavior, their compliance encourages their manager to continue to use the tactic, further complicating their relationship with their manager.

In both cases it would help the cause of the team member targeted by their manager if they find something to say in response to the adversarial behavior *at the time it occurs*, something that clarifies their reaction to the adversarial tactic. The main character needs to make it clear that they fully understand what they are being asked to do or to turn a blind eye to. Let's revisit the short examples and see how the team members involved could have handled them differently and better.

■ When her boss asks her to research the amount of time off her peer has had in the past six months, her team member tells her that she will do the task as requested. But she also says that she will inform the relevant colleague that she has been asked to find out this information. This is a clever thing to do. She makes it clear that she is cooperating with her manager in carrying out a specific task, but by telling her colleague what she is being asked to do, she prevents herself from being accused of colluding with her manager should her boss subsequently want to use the information against her colleague, or to use her involvement in the task against her. Furthermore, it clarifies to her boss that her team member holds some reservations about performing the task, reservations that she is sufficiently concerned about that she will act on them and make the request public. This one action prevents her boss from believing that she has 'bought' her, and preserves her autonomy in her relationship with her manager and her peer.

■ When the two peers realize that their boss has asked them both to carry out exactly the same project simultaneously, they go together to their boss. They say that *they are both confused* and need clarification about which of them is to carry out the project. They put forward the view that only one of them ought to carry out the work, and then ask their manager to select which of them he thinks is better qualified to handle it. They tell him that they will abide by his decision and leave it with him. This is a clever thing to do. By handling things this way, the two peers preserve their working relationship. They take responsibility for the muddled situation away from their boss, even though it is of his making, and present him with *their* confusion for *his* resolution. They ask him to make a decision to clarify the way forward, and so enable him to save face. They actually unmask their boss's game in trying to set up a competition between them, but do so in a way which respects his position as their manager, and his consequent right to choose which of his team members he wants to work on which project. But they also save themselves from carrying out duplicate work, and prevent their boss from setting them up in competition against one another.

In each of these situations the team member finds a way to protect themself from the repercussions of being seen to comply unwisely with their manager's adversarial behavior. In each of these situations their ability to do this effectively is predicated on their:

■ Willingness to say something back to their manager that clarifies the boundaries around what they will and what they won't do.
■ Capacity to present those boundaries in an open, non-confrontational but clear way.
■ Readiness to respect the ultimate authority of their manager, handing over to them decisions that rightly sit with them.

YOUR ADVERSARIAL COLLEAGUES

You may now like to take a moment to apply the material from the second half of this chapter to your own working life. You can jot down your answers to the following questions in the space below:

■ Identify a situation in which a manager used adversarial behavior with you and put you in an awkward position. What did they do or say that was uncomfortable for you?

◼ How did you handle this situation at the time? What impact did this way of handling things subsequently have on you and your work?

◼ Looking back on it now, what could you have done differently and better to handle this situation?

We have been examining a range of ways of protecting yourself from adversarial behavior in your manager. Let's now return to Case Study 17 earlier in this chapter, and see how that scenario is resolved. We left the action at the point at which a management team member is considering how to respond to her boss's request for a 'straight answer to a straight question.' The question posed to her asks her to give a view on whether a peer of hers, someone with whom she has been working closely for some time, is or is not up to the task of managing the company's new store.

CASE STUDY 19: KEEPING YOUR EYE ON THE BALL

The team member has a split second in which to determine how to answer the question her adversarial manager has just put to her. She decides that her only criterion for providing her answer will be her best understanding of the role she is employed to carry out. She tells her manager that she is employed to promote the company, and that her role as marketing manager involves her in a number of company-wide initiatives. She then says that during the course of her duties she has had the opportunity to assess the skills and performance of many of the management team members, including the colleague about whom she has just been asked. She informs her boss that, in her opinion as a marketing manager, any of the current management team including herself could make the step across to managing the new store. Then she says she is going to make a coffee, and as she sets off towards the kitchen, offers to make one for her manager.

Keeping Your Eye on the Ball: Analyzing the Dynamics

Let's revisit this situation to analyze the dynamics in it. In this scenario a management team member has to decide how to reply to her adversarial manager's tricky question about a peer's capacity to manage the company's new store. The management team member realizes that whether she answers 'Yes, he is up to the job' or 'No, he is not up to the job,' it will have repercussions for:

- Whether or not *she* is asked to manage the store.
- The quality of her relationship with her peer.
- Her manager's perception of her, her integrity, and her character.
- The extent to which her manager chooses to employ similar adversarial tactics with her in future.

She decides to change the point of the conversation away from the trap of a yes or no response, and it's a challenge that she handles well. She decides that she will only reply on the basis of her interpretation of her job role. She is the marketing manager, so her response as marketing manager will be honest, fair, and full. She will not be drawn into commenting directly on the abilities and skills of her peer. She will not be easily maneuvered into making an unguarded reply to a question she thinks both ill-considered and reprehensible. So she frames her answer only in terms of her specialism, and leaves her manager with a straight answer to a straight question, but without the kind of answer she was expecting.

Her answer is that as a marketing manager she has ample opportunity to observe her peers performing their roles, and her view is that many of the management team could step up and effectively manage the new store. This answer treads a careful balance between:

- Avoiding the trap of being seen to collude with her manager's adversarial game by speaking against her peer.
- Avoiding the trap of exceeding her own authority and giving a view on the performance of a peer when she isn't in a position to do so.
- Clarifying the boundaries within which she is prepared to give an opinion, which is as the marketing manager.
- Giving a fair and honest answer to the question put to her.
- Making it clear that she believes she would also be able to step up to the new role of store manager.
- Keeping the tone light and positive.
- Ending the exchange with an offer of a cup of coffee to signal that she is considers the conversation to be over, but in a pleasant way.

This is a useful answer to give. It keeps the team member firmly on safe ground. She speaks as the marketing manager about issues that she is both qualified and competent to discuss. She avoids getting into hot water by speaking out of turn about a peer, or by giving a view in the hope of its being the one her boss might want to hear. She succeeds in providing an answer, and a good one at that, but sidesteps the invitation to undermine a colleague or try to cozy up to her tricky boss. She maintains her integrity and strengthens her hand with her boss, who now knows that she cannot easily inveigle this particular team member into colluding with her against another member of the firm. In this instance, the management team member successfully dodges a tricky situation and a duplicitous question, but she will have to be on the look out for subsequent different adversarial tactics on part of her relentless manager.

KEEP ON DOING WHAT YOU USUALLY DO

You find yourself working for an adversarial manager. You haven't been in this position before, but now you are. When the shock of the situation dissipates you take stock. Faced with a level of continuous or intermittent subliminal or actual aggression from your adversarial manager, you may be tempted to:

- Think that your usual way of handling yourself at work won't be effective any more.
- Find a new way of doing things in the workplace, one that will be

more effective at protecting you from your manager's tactics than your usual, more relaxed style.

■ Adopt different ways of doing things, ones at which you are not as skilled or practised, and not as effective, all in an attempt to evade attack.

You can end up feeling that to protect yourself you need to do *everything* differently, not just when you are in a meeting with your adversarial manager, but in all your workplace activities and relationships. Depending on the ferocity of your manager, you can end up thinking that your usual workplace modus operandi won't do it, and that you need to develop a new suite of skills and behaviors to help you function and cope.

I hope this book will have helped you with some ideas about what those behaviors might consist of, and you will have other ideas of your own. But it is important to keep in mind that you can carry on doing what you normally do when you are not in the presence of your manager. You can carry on performing your role exactly as you used to before you worked for an adversarial boss. You don't have to expend energy adopting different behaviors at work in the hope of avoiding flak. It won't work and you will become less effective. You will run the risk of draining yourself as you look for 'new' and 'better' behaviors to use in the workplace, behaviors that will inevitably be unnatural for you to use, and time-consuming and energy-sapping to assimilate. You may find that, if you go down this route, you take your eye off your strengths and start to underperform in a role you are more than capable of handling well.

Instead, you can simply carry on doing what you normally do, attending to your tasks and duties that fall to you with the same level of attention and dedication you normally bring to them. Just because your manager is now an adversarial one and uses specific oppositional tactics doesn't mean that you have to change your way of doing things wholesale. You can continue to handle yourself, in the main, exactly as you always do, albeit with your eyes wide open when you encounter your manager and with an expectation that, at these times, you will likely need to employ strategies and tactics designed to be effective when handling an adversarial boss. You can also keep an eye out for signals that your adversarial manager is trying to play you off against other members of the workforce, and act accordingly when you encounter these tactics. *At these times,* by all means utilize ideas you may have gained from this book and ideas of your own, to help you manage your interaction with your manager and peers. But at all other times carry on as you usually would.

SUMMARY AND NEXT CHAPTER

This chapter has focused on a number of ways to engage productively with an adversarial manager, someone who has an oppositional mindset and significant organizational authority. The key message of the chapter has been that it is up to you to find ways of demonstrating respect for your manager's *position* while politely but firmly clarifying the *boundaries* under which you are comfortable to work.

The chapter has highlighted the particular values and tactics employed by adversarial managers. It has described the mindset of an adversarial manager, and illustrated how differently an adversarial manager uses the power available to them in their role in comparison with a non-adversarial manager. The chapter has suggested that adversarial managers assess their team members on a continuum that includes their ability to stand up to intimidation, their ability to respect the authority of the manager, and their ability to handle adversarial tactics effectively. The chapter has highlighted the pitfalls inherent in complying with the wishes of an adversarial manager out of fear, or getting angry with them and opposing them on instinct. It presented a number of ways in which to handle adversarial tactics in a manager, including hearing undermining openings as a signal that your manager has something to say, presenting your preferences and wishes as a service to your boss, being prepared to lose less, clarifying your reaction to adversarial tactics at the time they are employed, clarifying what you are prepared to do and what you are not prepared to do, and interacting with your manager solely on the basis of your best understanding of your role. The chapter presented the view that it is in your best interests to remain committed to your usual ways of handling yourself at work when you are not in a meeting with your manager, and avoid the temptation to make wholesale changes to the way in which you handle yourself in the workplace in a misguided attempt to protect yourself.

The next chapter continues to explore the themes of the handling adversarial managers but changes tack in that it takes the form of a narrative case study. The case study gives you an opportunity to read the action, apply the material from this and previous chapters of the book to it, and decide how you would handle the evolving issues. The case study follows the fortunes of an employee of a fictional clothing manufacturer who is promoted to work for the company's top team. The managers in the top team arrange their relationships with one another as a series of adversarial alliances, a state of affairs that creates a highly political and challenging environment for the newly promoted employee to get to grips with. The case study focuses in particular on his relationship with one adversarial senior manager, and illustrates how the newly promoted employee handles this colleague's inimical nature.

CHAPTER 8

Adversarial Allies

A Narrative Case Study

The following case study is an opportunity for you to analyze an evolving adversarial situation in a fictional workplace and determine how you could respond to the action as it develops. In the case study an employee is promoted to the post of training manager to work with the top team in a fictional clothing manufacturer. The challenges before him include navigating the political alliances among the top team members and finding ways of working effectively with an increasingly adversarial senior manager. The case study focuses on the relationships between the newly promoted training manager, one of his new internal clients, the brand manager, and his boss, the sales director.

As you read the case study you will see that the narrative is presented in sections. Following each portion you will find a set of questions to answer, questions that give you the opportunity to delve behind the action and analyze the deeper dynamics at play between the main characters. You can jot down your answers to these questions in the space following each one, and can subsequently compare your answers with those you will find at the end of the chapter.

MOVING UP

An ambitious and talented training adviser in a clothing manufacturer is offered the chance to step up to the role of training manager. His new role involves him in running the team he had been a part of, and despite the complexity of becoming manager to his erstwhile peers, he accepts the challenge readily. The main task facing him and his team of six is to design and deliver the subsequent year's training and development program for the company.

The new training manager is slightly daunted at the prospect of working with the top team members in the firm. While he regards his promotion as a big pat on the back, he is also aware of the highly political relationships that exist among some of the senior people in the clothing manufacturer. Not by nature that politically minded or that comfortable in adversarial alliances, but by no means either naïve or reluctant either, the new training manager nonetheless looks forward to his new role, and sets about the tasks before him enthusiastically.

During his first week in his new job he and his team devise a program of research to enable them to understand the training requirements of their key internal clients, the top team. One of these managers is the brand manager, an experienced and energetic man in his mid-40s who has an enormous capacity for taking on and tackling work. The brand manager arrives for work before 6.30 am every day and often leaves after 7 pm. He is creative and determined, and provided that his team members don't question his authority or his judgment too loudly, he is a reasonably fair man to work for. But the brand manager is a jealous man and a tricky team member to deal with, someone capable of appearing charming and open when it suits him, while handling things in a different way behind the scenes. He is also aware that his team is not as efficient or as effective as it should be, and that some of his top team colleagues think it is actually underperforming.

The brand manager reports to the sales director, who is two years his senior. She is diminutive, feisty, and effective at creating opportunities to promote the clothing company's lines throughout its primary marketplace, which is the Far East and China. The brand manager and the sales director have an occasionally explosive, sometimes tense relationship which works because each of them rates the other's technical abilities. In matters of sales or brand management each is prepared to defer to the other's judgment, and the brand manager is sensible enough not to disagree with his boss in open forum. The sales director reports directly to the CEO, with whom she has an effective if slightly distant relationship.

The brand manager joined the company two and a half years previously. having been poached by the sales director from a rival company. During the period in which the two of them have worked together the clothing manufacturer's turnover has doubled.

MEETING THE SENIOR TEAM

During his first week the training manager and his team also review the previous year's training activity and devise a priority list of development initiatives to put to the top team. The training manager has a special interest in developing and working with teams. He hopes that he will be able to use his skills and experience to improve the quality of teamwork demonstrated by many of the company's teams. The training manager takes the decision that he alone will carry out the forthcoming research interviews with the top team members in the company. He regards this round of meetings as an opportunity for him to establish credibility with his new internal clients, as well as an opportunity to see how the land lies politically between them. He arranges eight one-hour discussions with each of the top team members including the CEO, the sales director and the brand manager.

The training manager meets the sales director first, and after ten minutes, is clear that he has established both liking and respect with her. The sales director speaks openly with him about her wish to grow the company, the key role that she envisages for training in that process, and her hope that the training manager will become a valued adviser to the senior team. She tells him that she likes the way he has conducted himself during his first few days in his new role, and that she would like him to report back to her after he has concluded his eight research meetings. The training manager takes these comments at face value, and is pleased that at least one member of the senior team has been, as he sees it, candid and positive about his early work.

The following week he meets with the brand manager and the CEO. The brand manager is also open with him, and apparently interested in his plans for the training provision in the company. Early on in the meeting the brand manager mentions that the sales director has already made positive noises about the training manager to a number of senior people in the company, including him. Then he says that in his opinion the meeting between the sales director and the training manager constituted a 'meeting of minds.'

The training manager is rather surprised at this characterization of the conversation he had with the sales director, especially as the brand manager wasn't at the meeting in question and is unlikely to know much about its content except for a brief summary from his boss. He certainly doesn't think that his one-hour conversation with the sales director constituted 'a meeting of minds,' and wonders what he is being told and why. However, some instinct for self-preservation prevents him from saying anything in return, and he lets the moment pass without comment. Instead he moves the conversation on by asking the brand manager what input he and his team would like from him in the next year. The training manager is again surprised when the brand manager tells him that he would like him to work with his team as soon as possible, and that he will get back to him later that week to discuss the details of the project with him.

Subsequently, the training manager meets with the CEO, whom he likes. He regards him as being an avuncular man with a keen sense of humor. The CEO asks him a number of insightful questions, then says that he understands he will be meeting with the sales director a second time. The training manager realizes that the sales director and the CEO have already talked about him, and decides that the tone of this conversation was probably favorable.

Having concluded the eight research interviews, the training manager arranges to meet the sales director again so that he can summarize his findings for her. During this discussion she invites him to the next senior team meeting, a twice-monthly event which the top eight managers in the company attend. The training manager is delighted to receive this invitation. He regards participating in this meeting as an opportunity to learn more about the political context at the top of the company while continuing with his plans to establish credibility with its senior players.

ATTENDING THE TOP TEAM MEETING

The training manager attends the senior meeting the following week, where he meets the CEO for the second time. He is surprised just how much the sales director monopolizes the meeting, and how uncreative it is. For much of its two hours, the majority of the people in the room remain silent. Only two or three people speak, and it is the sales director who holds the floor most of all. The training manager runs his own team meetings along different lines, encouraging debate and discussion from everyone around the table. He notices that the brand manager doesn't interact with any of the people in the room and apart from saying hello and swapping pleasantries with him, doesn't engage with him either.

Towards the end of the meeting the sales director raises the issue of growing the company's turnover still further over the next two years. She says that she wants to set a goal that the company will increase its turnover by 50 percent in the next 24 months. She adds that, as far as she is concerned, training and development will be a key factor in the company attaining this goal. She then invites the training manager to outline his research conclusions following his recent round of talks with people present. The training manager outlines his key findings, and explains that he would like to combine a targeted series of training interventions with work to improve team performance across the company. He expects the brand manager to come in at this point and volunteer that he, the brand manager, has asked the training manager to work with his team. But the brand manager remains silent, and the training manager decides not to disclose the fact that they have discussed the project.

The meeting closes with the training manager pleased to have been given the opportunity to address the meeting but slightly unnerved by some its dynamics. He returns to his office and briefs his team on the role they will play in supporting the sales director to achieve her goal of a 50 percent improvement in the company's turnover over the next two years.

QUESTIONS FOR YOU TO ANSWER: SET ONE

Thinking about the action from the point of view of the training manager answer the following three questions:

■ The brand manager tells the training manager that there has been a 'meeting of minds' between him and the sales director. What could be his motive for saying this?

■ The training manager is perturbed by some of the dynamics in the top team meeting. What in particular would he do well to note?

■ At this early stage what clues are there about the brand manager's adversarial nature that the training manager needs to be aware of?

WORKING WITH THE BRAND TEAM

Following the top team meeting the training manager and the brand manager sit down to discuss the team project that the brand manager wants him to run for the brand team. They agree a plan of work that will involve the training manager meeting one-to-one with each member of the team before running a half-day team assessment workshop to measure their performance across a series of key indicators. Two days later the training manager receives an email from the brand manager, in which the brand manager suggests some additional outcomes he would like to see from the workshop. He says that he would like to see greater willingness on the part of his team members to disagree with him and challenge his thinking in team meetings, plus more innovative and creative ideas originating from them. He complains that he ends up doing most of the talking at team meetings, and that while his team are assiduous at implementing his ideas, they don't initiate enough of their own.

The training manager forms the view that the reluctance of the brand team to initiate new ideas is likely to be down to the management style of the brand manager. He decides to check out this theory during his research with the brand team. He hypothesizes that the slightly authoritarian, formal, and closed style of the brand manager precludes openness or risk taking in the team, and results in his team members failing to innovate or be creative in case they get something wrong and incur the displeasure of their boss. Having had first-hand experience of the side of the brand manager which results in him making comments simply to see what effect they will have, the training manager wonders if the brand manager isn't also capable of using trickery and manipulation with his own staff. He makes a mental note to enquire of the brand team members what happens when something goes wrong in the team, and under what circumstances the brand manager might feel the need to tick one of them off. He also decides to ask them what he might hear the brand manager saying and observe him doing should he feel the need to provide anyone in the team with negative feedback.

The research interviews prove particularly interesting to the training manager. He hears anecdotal evidence of the brand manager conveying disapproval of individual members of the team in team meetings, seemingly in circumstances where the misdemeanor doesn't warrant a public reprimand. He also hears anecdotal evidence of the brand manager being too forceful with some people in the team, and not listening sufficiently well to others. All in all the training manager is not surprised that creativity is low, and that brand team members find it difficult to contradict or challenge their sometimes unreasonable and tactless manager.

The training manager decides that the most useful way to handle these dynamics is during the event itself. He is aware of the political sensitivity surrounding the impact of the brand manager's style on his team members, and wants *them* to tell *him* about these issues themselves. He sees his role as that of facilitating the workshop well enough that at least one team member feels comfortable enough to broach this subject with his boss, in which case he as facilitator could encourage discussion of the point raised and bring other people in. He finalizes the process he wants to use during the event, and then designs the slides that display the findings from his research.

LAST-MINUTE HITCH

But late in the day on the evening before the team assessment workshop, and just as he is about to sign off for the day, the team manager receives an email from the brand manager. It is entitled 'workshop,' and informs the training manager that the brand manager has some concerns about the planned event. He lists three of them, namely that he doesn't see where the workshop is going, is worried that it won't achieve its goals, and thinks it might be too much about him, the brand manager. The training manager is annoyed at the tone, content, and timing of the email. The brand manager has not raised any of these issues with him previously, and the training manager thinks it is too late for him to raise them the evening before the event, especially on email. He send back a reply which says that he is looking forward to the workshop, shuts down his computer, and goes home.

Nevertheless the training manager is worried. He is aware of the sensitive dynamic that exists between him and the brand manager. On the one hand the brand manager has paid him a compliment by asking him to work with his team so soon after his promotion, but on the other hand he recognizes that the brand manager is also a tricky customer to deal with. Although the brand manager hasn't said anything directly to confirm this opinion, the training manager forms the view that the sales director is putting him and his team under pressure to achieve more quickly, presumably so that she can hit her target of adding 50 percent to the company's turnover in the space of the next two years. The training manager thinks that the anxiety revealed by the brand manager in his email is actually a reflection of his wider concerns about fulfilling the sales director's expectations of him. The training manager decides to tread carefully in the workshop. He decides that the sensitivities in his relationship with the brand manager are such that he could lose his status as his valued internal adviser quite quickly if he mishandles the following day's events.

QUESTIONS FOR YOU TO ANSWER: SET TWO

Thinking about the action from the point of view of the brand manager, answer the following two questions:

- The brand manager asks the training manager to work with his team soon after his appointment is made. What factors prompt him to select the newly promoted training manager to carry out this role as opposed to an external facilitator?

- What is going through the mind of the brand manager when he sends his last-minute email to the training manager?

Thinking about the action from the point of view of the training manager, answer the following question:

- What risk is the training manager taking by accepting the project with the brand team so soon after taking on his new role?

THE TEAM ASSESSMENT WORKSHOP

The team assessment event starts at 11 am. By lunchtime the atmosphere in the room is tense. The training manager struggles to get any substantial dialogue going, and has to do a lot of talking himself. He wants to focus the morning around a discussion of the interpersonal issues the team needs to talk about. Instead he spends more time than he wants feeding back his assessment of the team's strengths and weaknesses, and then has to spend considerable time trying to create an atmosphere in which at least one of the team will risk telling the truth about the impact of the brand manager's style on the quality of their work and relationships. It is hard going at times, but the training manager thinks that by lunchtime he is making progress. When he calls a break for lunch, the brand manager comes over to talk to him. The brand manager tells the training manager that the morning has been 'boring.' The training manager is surprised at this characterization. He thinks it odd that the manager of a team thinks a two-hour discussion about that team is 'boring.' He also disagrees. He doesn't think the workshop has been boring, it has been more edgy and uptight, but he also thinks that is has made progress. He asserts his view that progress has been made, and rather than get into a discussion about his difference of perception with the brand manager, he says he needs to eat, and goes to get a sandwich.

The afternoon session is more eventful. Soon after the restart one of the more senior members of the team ventures the opinion that the team could produce more if it was arranged differently. He suggests that the role of team leader could be more outward facing, and that the team itself could report to two of its more senior team members rather than the brand manager. This would enable the brand manager to spend more time with retail outlets and clients, assessing their requirements and building customer loyalty, rather than managing the day-to-day work of the team. The team could then focus on initiating and managing projects along geographical lines, with one half focusing on the Chinese market and the second half concentrating on their other Far Eastern markets. The training manager asks the brand manager for his reaction to this suggestion. The following interaction is vehement. The brand manager says he needs to understand the ins and outs of the suggestion, which is one he was not expecting, and asks why he hasn't heard about it before. The team member who volunteered the suggestion says that it isn't easy raising issues with him, and that, as the workshop is specifically being held to look for performance improvements, this is as good a time as any.

The training manager lets this dialogue develop without comment. The brand manager then directs a remark to him. He says that he should be managing the debate more closely, and should not be letting it move onto issues that cannot be concluded in the two hours that remain. From this point onwards the training manager spends less time facilitating the process, and the team members speak more than him. The workshop concludes with the team having a clear view of its strengths and weaknesses, but not having a clear view of the way forward with regard to either a potential new structure or how to address performance weaknesses.

When he finally draws the meeting to a close the training manager is surprised to see the brand manager approach him with a broad smile on his face. He thanks him, saying that 'The exercise has been useful,' before leaving to return to his office. The training manager makes a mental note to speak with him the following day about the issue of a new structure for the team. He considers that given the brand manager's style of handling his team, the idea is worth pursuing, but also thinks that the brand manager needs more time to get used to the suggestion so he can understand fully its ramifications before agreeing to take it forward.

QUESTIONS FOR YOU TO ANSWER: SET THREE

Thinking about the action from the point of view of the training manager, answer the following question:

▪ The brand manager characterizes the morning of the workshop as 'boring,' and reacts quite strongly to the afternoon suggestion that the team adopt a new structure. However at the end of the meeting he is all smiles. What could account for his changed demeanor?

SIX QUESTIONS

On arriving at work the following morning the training manager downloads his emails. He notices one from the sales director, which he opens immediately. It is entitled 'Six questions,' and contains a series of punchy statements followed by six probing questions. The statements convey the view that the brand team workshop held the previous day was not well facilitated and went off course. The six questions hold him accountable for his failure to research the issues fully, his failure to manage the process to a suitable conclusion, his decision to continue with a meandering process after lunch, his failure to provide the team's leader with a heads up about discussions on a potential new structure for the team, and his failure to use the time of an entire team full of people effectively at a juncture in the company's development when it needs to push forward, not waste time.

The training manager is stunned. His mind reels as he tries to fill in the blanks between the brand manager's friendly and positive departure from the workshop the previous day and this email. Without any facts to go on, all he can do is speculate about what reports the sales director has had about the event, and from whom. He thinks through his options, and picks up the phone to call the brand manager.

The brand manager is in his office, and sounds relaxed when he speaks with the training manager. The training manager doesn't mention the email he has just read, but instead asks the brand manager whether he has a chance to give the sales director a report about the workshop. The brand manager replies that he has given her a full account of the discussions at the workshop. This answer doesn't really provide the training manager with the response he was looking for, so he presses further. He asks the brand manager what kind of report he provided to the sales director. The brand manager says that he thought the workshop had some positive aspects to it. The training manager hears the equivocation in this reply, and forms the silent view that the brand manager also thinks the workshop had some downsides to it, downsides which he did not share with him at the end of the process when he smilingly said it had been a useful exercise. He counters by reminding the brand manager of these parting words. The brand manager responds with the line 'Everything in business has value,' before he points out that he has a meeting to go to and ends the call. The call ends with the training manager feeling distinctly uncomfortable.

The training manager looks back at the sales director's email and reads it again. He doesn't even know if the brand manager is aware that the sales director has sent it. He is also conscious that up until this point the sales director has always been positive about him and his work. He composes himself and drafts a reply. In his response he is careful not to criticize the brand manager. He defends his handling of the research and his facilitation of the event, before saying that he thinks the complaint made against him is an over-reaction and is not consistent with the facts. He says that the workshop made progress, and that the debate was tense at times but never counter-productive. He points out that the brand team is not used to having open discussions with one another or with their manager, and that they took time to get used to doing this. He states that the team members and the team leader now have a clear view of the team's strengths and areas for development, and have a potentially beneficial new structure to discuss. He says that as a result of the workshop the team members and the brand manager have had conversations they would not have otherwise had, conversations which they can continue themselves thereafter. He concedes that there is still work to be done in the team, but says that this is not a failing of the workshop, more a reflection of how it is. He ends by saying that the brand manager was positive about the workshop at the conclusion of the event, that the training manager thinks it has added value to the team's work, and that the sales director could refer to any of the other team members who participated in the workshop if she wants to supplement her current point of view. Then he sends the email and waits for a response.

After two hours in which he does not receive a reply, the training manager calls the sales director's office and asks to speak to her. Her PA tells him that she has seen his email, is in meetings all day, and will get back to him in due course. The training manager finds it difficult to concentrate on his work that day. He worries about what the sales director now thinks of him, feels anxious in case she has communicated her negative view about his work to other top team members, and has a growing sense of unease about the role of the brand manager in events since the close of the workshop. He goes home at 6 o'clock without having heard anything back from the sales director, and without having any further communications with the brand manager.

QUESTIONS FOR YOU TO ANSWER: SET FOUR

Thinking about the action from the point of view of the training manager answer the following two questions:

- The training manager is in a tricky position politically. What are the key factors for him to take into account as he considers his next move?

■ The training manager could have used his telephone call with the brand manager to confront him about what role he played in helping to form the sales director's adverse view of the workshop. What factors dissuade him from adopting this course of action?

PICKING UP THE PIECES

The training manager arrives at work the following day feeling very out of sorts. After an evening's reflection he decides that the sales director's negative view of the team assessment workshop is wholly down to the brand manager. He doesn't understand why the brand manager has acted against him, and having formed the view that the he deliberately presented a false picture of the workshop to his boss for reasons which only he will understand, feels angered and duped. The training manager becomes more and more angry during the day. He twice re-reads the sales director's email and then re-reads his own response. Twice he picks up the telephone to call the sales director again, and twice changes his mind. His team members note his mood and stay clear of him, only coming to him for input on urgent issues that need his attention.

The training manager is particularly cross at the fact that he had thought that he and the brand manager, while very different people, were working together towards a common aim: that of improving the brand team's performance. His view was that the brand manager needed his input to improve his team, and that he needed the opportunity to prove himself an effective training manager, an opportunity that the brand manager provided for him. He was grateful that the brand manager asked him to carry out the project so soon after his promotion, but now he thinks that his openness to the brand manager was misguided. He begins to see the brand manager as a clever, inimical character, one who has purposefully taken him in and set him up for a fall. He doesn't feel able to go and confront him because he has nothing concrete to go on. Furthermore, he doesn't think a confrontation will get him anywhere. He thinks he will sound paranoid if he comes out with his suspicions. He feels increasingly frustrated at the position he finds himself in, one in which he cannot resolve anything with the sales director nor find out exactly what has gone on in the brand manager's head. He fears for his reputation with the wider senior team and the CEO. Towards the end of the day he goes to the sales director's office to speak with her, and is told that she has left for the day.

For his part the brand manager behaves quite normally with his team. He decides to discuss the ins and outs of the proposed new structure with them, and sets up a meeting to do this. He excludes the training manager from the meeting, which he asks the team member who originated the idea to facilitate. He tells the sales director in an email that he is picking up the pieces left by the workshop, and aims to turn negatives into positives.

QUESTIONS FOR YOU TO ANSWER: SET FIVE

Thinking about the action from the point of view of the brand manager, answer the following two questions:

■ What does the brand manager hope to gain by handling things in this way?

■ What risks does the brand manager take in handling things as he does?

THE SALES DIRECTOR'S RESPONSE

A whole week passes, and the training manager still hears nothing from the sales director. He and his team work on the development of their targeted training initiatives. Late on Friday evening he receives an email from the sales director's PA entitled 'Top team meeting,' in which she says that the sales director would like him to attend the next top team meeting on the following Tuesday afternoon. She makes no mention of the sales director's previous email, the training manager's reply, or the outstanding issues between them.

The training manager is worried. Various scenarios run through his mind, none of which is comfortable for him. He imagines being publicly upbraided at the meeting or being asked to account for his handling of the team assessment workshop in front of the top team. He imagines having to chat to the brand manager at the start of the meeting, and doesn't know how he will handle that encounter, or what he will say to him. He doesn't know what reports any of the other top team members have had about the workshop or his handling of it, and he can no longer be sure that the CEO regards him favorably. He decides to send an email back to the sales director's PA asking what input he is expected to make to the meeting. She replies 30 minutes later saying that he is being invited to the meeting but adding nothing further. The training manager spends an uncomfortable few days leading up the top team meeting, which he attends as requested.

FALLOUT

On his return to his office after participating in the top team meeting the training manager has a number of issues to attend to. He needs to prepare for a presentation to the CEO, sales director, and brand manager at the end of the week. His presentation will outline his plans for rolling out the targeted training initiative throughout the company. He needs to submit a précis of his plans to them all 24 hours before the presentation, and be prepared to start the rollout two weeks earlier than planned.

The training manager is not asked to speak at the top team meeting. Instead he hears debate and discussions about a number of issues concerning the company's last and subsequent quarter's performance. The brand manager is distant but cordial with him, and the sales director only speaks to him once, which is to acknowledge that he has arrived. He listens during the meeting and when it closes he leaves. At no point does he feel put on the spot, singled out, or particularly included in or excluded from the meeting. Nonetheless, he leaves with much to do, and as all of it is in line with his job description, he forms the view that the fallout from the team assessment workshop has settled, and gets on with his work. Instead of trying to resolve the issues between him and the sales director he decides to reframe the situation as a successful although unexpected damage limitation exercise. He has learned a lot from his encounters with the brand manager and the sales director, and with his eyes wide open, sets about rolling out an effective training initiative with his team.

QUESTIONS FOR YOU TO ANSWER: SET SIX

Thinking about the action from the point of view of the brand manager, answer the following four questions:

■ What is your reading of the situation in which the training manager now finds himself?

■ Although he didn't know it at the time, the training manager's handling of his email exchange with the sales director helped his cause. What aspects of his writing style helped him sway her opinion of the workshop?

■ How does the training manager's handling of his relationship with the brand manager work in his favor?

■ What could the training manager have done differently and better from the time he gained his promotion onwards which might have rendered him less vulnerable to the tactics of an adversarial ally?

REVIEW SECTION: ANSWERS TO THE QUESTIONS

The final section of the case study provides a summary of the key issues in it. Each of the bullet points below relates, in order, to one of the questions above. You might like to read each answer and compare it with the notes that you jotted down.

Set One

■ The brand manager tells the training manager that there has been a 'meeting of minds' between him and the sales director. What could be his motive for saying this?

The brand manager tests the training manager by saying something that is at once untrue but which he thinks the training manager might like to hear as someone new into his post. He plays with the training manager to see how he will react, and what he can learn about his weaknesses. He hopes that by using the phrase 'a meeting of minds' he will give the training manager cause to believe that he has established a greater degree of influence with the sales director than is actually the case. The brand manager does this because he wants to know how much the training manager needs the approval of the sales director, and to what extent he might be prepared to reveal this vulnerability should he in fact possess it. As it happens the training manager isn't fooled and actually doesn't really believe the comment. But he doesn't go that one step further and hear it as the red flag it is. He wonders what could have motivated the brand manager to make this remark, and wrongly concludes that the brand manager has made a mistake and misinterpreted his embryonic relationship with the sales director. So he fails to hear the warning these mischievous words actually represent. He would have done better to have taken note of the comment and ask what the brand manager meant. He could have said something like 'I'm not with you' or 'You've lost me,' and waited for a response. Whatever the reply, and it is by no means certain that a skilled operator like the brand manager would have given an explicit one, the training manager needs to be on the lookout for similar warnings in his subsequent dealings with him. However, there is a second reason why the brand manager makes the comment about 'a meeting of minds.' It makes him sound relaxed that the new kid on the block might have caught the favorable attention of his boss the sales director. By saying this so early in his relationship with the training manager and with apparently so little effort, he wishes to create the impression in the mind of the training manager that he is not at all put out by his newly found favor with his boss. This is in fact a smokescreen, because he has noted the positive things that the sales director as said about the training manager with some considerable chagrin and annoyance.

■   The training manager is perturbed by some of the dynamics in the top team meeting. What in particular would he do well to note?

The first thing for him to note is that the sales director holds the floor for much of the meeting. This suggests that she has a significant need to exert power over the group, enough that she wishes to command the attention of the meeting for considerable periods of time. It also suggests that a number of people in the room, whether consciously or unconsciously, allow her to dominate the meeting, possibly because they can then coast and take a back seat, or because they are reluctant to take her on even though she is not the most senior person in the room. Second, he needs to take note of the fact that, although she dominates the meeting, the sales director is not the most senior person in the room. The CEO is, and he allows the sales director free rein in this forum. This suggests that the CEO and sales director have found a way to work together that results in the sales director being allowed to indulge her need to dominate the top team meeting, and while the training manager won't know the ins and outs of their alliance, he can reasonably conclude that the CEO extends some considerable latitude to his sales director in this forum. Third, the training manager needs to note that the brand manager doesn't mix that well with anyone in the room. He is quite standoffish and doesn't engage with his colleagues informally. Nor does he contribute that much to the formal discussions. He does say hello to the training manager when he arrives in the meeting room, but doesn't chat to him, even though the brand manager has asked the training manager to work with his team, and has already met him one-to-one. Fourth, during the meeting the brand manager has an ideal opening to volunteer to his colleagues that he has asked the training manager to work with his team. But he doesn't take up this option, preferring to keep the information to himself, and thereby creating the impression that he doesn't want the top team to know about the project. Fortunately, the training manager is savvy enough to keep his mouth shut and let the moment pass without comment.

■ At this early stage what clues are there about the brand manager's adversarial nature that the training manager needs to be aware of?

The problem facing the training manager is that while there are hints that he might be quite a tricky customer, at this stage there are no obvious clues to the extent of the adversarial nature of the brand manager. The main clue to his oppositional and devious disposition is the brand manager's comment about a 'meeting of minds' between the training manager and the sales director, but this comment alone is insufficient to cause the training manager to regard him as an adversarial character. The training manager can say with some certainty that the brand manager wants a high degree of control over what perceptions his top team colleagues form about him and his team, but this is not unusual, and is not a sign of him being particularly untrustworthy, unsupportive, or hostile towards his colleague.

Set Two

■ The brand manager asks the training manager to work with his team soon after his appointment is made. What factors prompt him to select the newly promoted training manager to carry out this role as opposed to an external facilitator?

The brand manager chooses the training manager to work with his team for a number of reasons, all of which involve a hidden benefit to him. He is nothing if not clever in the way he goes about it. He could have hired an external facilitator to carry out this important piece of work, or he could have delayed the project for a few months until the training manager had found his feet in his new role. But instead the brand manager asks him to carry out the work straight after his promotion. Of course, this could be because he is under serious pressure from the sales director and needs to act to improve his team's performance straightaway. And it could also be because he has sufficient faith in the training manager's reputation and appointment that he doesn't think it premature to ask him to carry out the work immediately. However, there is another reason for his speedy decision to ask the training manager to handle this important project. It places the training manager, as far as the brand manager is concerned, in his power, and provides him with an opportunity to look for ways in which to act against him should he wish to. Being new into the role and unused to dealing with the senior managers in the company, the training manager is both keen to prove himself and vulnerable. The brand manager realizes this, and calculates that the training manager is likely to jump at an early chance to work with the brand team and prove to at least one of his new internal clients that he is the right man for the job. The brand manager also judges that, given the role that the sales director wants training to play in the company over the next two years, any opportunity for the training manager to forge closer links with one of the top team will be one he will welcome. And so it proves. The training manager accepts the option of working with the brand team, and the first part of the brand manager's plan has fallen into place. He has moved the training manager into a position where is closer to him, a position where the training manager will feel that he is trusted. He has already told the training manager that there is a 'meeting of minds' between him and the sales director, partly to make it look as if he is sufficiently on the side of the training manager and sufficiently relaxed with himself that he can afford to pass on positive feedback to him. The brand manager hopes that the training manager will be sufficiently naïve and sufficiently blind to the political reality at the top of the company that he will fail to realize he is being maneuvered, and will regard the brand manager as an ally, so providing him with more room within which to manipulate should he subsequently need it.

■   What is going through the mind of the brand manager when he sends his last-minute email to the training manager?

The brand manager genuinely has last-minute nerves, but doesn't handle them very well. He doesn't pick up the phone during the day and call the training manager to talk through the growing number of issues running through his mind. He waits until the last minute, and faced with the prospect of going home and worrying, sends an ineffective email raising big issues at the end of the day. He is worried that the event won't go well, but it's not for the reasons he gives. His choice of stated concerns – that he doesn't see where the workshop is going, is worried that it won't achieve its goals, and thinks it might be too much about him, the brand manager – are smokescreens designed to mask the real issue. The real issue is his genuine concern that his team might speak openly about his flaws as a manager. He is a talented brand manager but not an able manager of people. His relationship with his team members is predicated on his requirement that they respect and bow to his authority, and when he perceives that they don't, or when he feels the need to reinforce the fact that he is the boss, he can be sharp and unpleasant. It is this adversarial side of his conduct with his team members that destroys creativity in the team, and reduces the enthusiasm and endeavor that they would otherwise be willing to display. The night before the workshop the brand manager gets last-minute nerves. He is worried that his carefully laid plans might go awry and that the naïve training manager might prove more effective at his job than he wants him to be. The brand manager needs to be seen to be addressing the issues in his team, hence the team assessment workshop. But he doesn't want the training manager to get too close to the truth in case it proves painful for him, so he suggests in his last-minute email that the workshop shouldn't focus on him too much, and that he can't quite see where it is going. Sadly, for him the training manager is not thrown by his email. If anything, he is annoyed by it. He sees it as an attempt to undermine him at the last minute and effectively ignores it. This is actually an error of judgment on the part of the training manager. He really needs to pick up the phone, even though it is late in the day, and talk to the brand manager. Leaving him simmering over night will only add to the possibility that he might misbehave at the event itself.

■ What risk is the training manager taking by accepting the project with the brand team so soon after taking on his new role?

The risk that the training manager is taking is not actually about how new in post he is as such. The main risk is related to the fact that it is the brand manager he is working for while he is still finding his feet in the new role. The project with the brand team is high profile. Even if the brand manager chooses not to disclose anything about it at the top team meeting, word will get out that the training manager is running a team improvement program for the brand team, and given that the brand and sales teams work closely together and are both important in improving the company's turnover figures, this is a piece of work which all the senior players in the company will be watching closely. The training manager is in a delicate position. Keen to prove himself a trusted internal supplier, and keen to undertake a project involving his specialism of improving teamwork, he accepts the brief and starts work on the project. He doesn't really consider the risks because he is unaware of the adversarial nature of his new internal client. He does know from his early dealings with him that the brand manager is a bit tricky to deal with and he knows from his research with his team that he runs his team in an authoritarian manner. But he doesn't know the full extent of the brand manager's duplicity or just how ruthless he can be and so is unprepared for the maneuver that he employs against him.

Set Three

■ The brand manager characterizes the morning of the workshop as 'boring,' and reacts quite strongly to the afternoon suggestion that the team adopts a new structure. However at the end of the meeting he is all smiles. What could account for his changed demeanor?

The brand manager wants to keep the training manager on his toes. He also wants to see how far he can push him before he snaps. He recognizes that the morning is a bit of a slog, so decides that the lunch break is an ideal opportunity to push the training manager for the first time. He walks over to the training manager and characterizes the workshop as 'boring.' Then he waits for a reaction. But he doesn't get one, and somewhat surprised, he hears the training manager disagree with this characterization before disengaging from the conversation and simply leaving the room. The brand manager makes a mental note to try to unsettle him again, this time after lunch. During the debate that follows the lunchtime break he genuinely does not like the suggestion that he should cease managing his team and allow two other people to share these duties while he spends more time working directly with clients. He decides that this proposal is a slight on his management skills, and given that the workshop is about identifying performance improvements, he also hears it as an oblique reference to the adverse effect he has on team morale. But it is also a useful second chance to have a dig at the training manager, this time in front of his team. He vehemently makes the point that he didn't know such a suggestion would be debated at the event, before attacking the training manager for allowing discussion of a large issue with insufficient time to debate it properly. However, by the end of the workshop he is sunny side up, and comments to the training manager that the workshop has been 'useful.' His changed demeanor is something that the training manager takes at face value, but a closer look reveals that this is not a sound view to take. The discussion during the final two hours of the workshop does not clarify either how the team will address its performance issues, or whether it will or won't adopt the new structure. There really is nothing for the brand manager to be smiling about. The workshop has raised key issues about his management style and the way his team is structured which it has not resolved, and he will need to address both sets of issues after the workshop, either with or without the involvement of the training manager. His smiling reaction is therefore out of synch with the mood of the meeting and his personal feelings at its conclusion. The training manager needs to notice this discrepancy and follow it up with the brand manager. He needs to ask him what he has found useful and why. He needs to ask him what he would like to happen next. He needs to find out what is going on in the brand manager's mind that could account for his smiling mood, and to question him to find out what involvement he would like from him going forward. By accepting at face value the comment that the event has been 'useful', even though it doesn't fit with the outcome of the meeting, the training manager allows himself to be lulled into a false sense of security.

Set Four

■ The training manager is in a tricky position politically. What are the key factors for him to take into account as he considers his next move?

The training manager does not know for sure who has said what to the sales director, although it is clear that the brand manager must have said something to her that he hasn't also said to him. Reading between the lines he is faced with two possibilities. First, the brand manager may be behaving in a duplicitous way. He may be playing it one way to the training manager's face when he tells him that the workshop has been useful, but then might have conveyed a different picture to his boss, the sales director. He may have given her a scathing description of the workshop, one which directly and solely leads her to send her email to the training manager without discussing any of the issues she addresses in it with him first. The second option is that the sales director does hear an accurate picture of the workshop from the brand manager but takes a different view about the value of the exercise. However, given her positive regard for the training manager up until this point, if she had any suspicions about the outcomes of the workshop she could reasonably have been expected to give him the benefit of the doubt and discuss the issues with him. Therefore it is more likely that the first option is in play, and that the sales director has sent a fierce email to a junior colleague out of the blue without having first given him an opportunity to talk through her concerns with her. Whatever has gone on behind the scenes, the training manager now has to answer six pithy questions, all of which are predicated on the premise that he has mishandled the brand team's teambuilding workshop.

- ■ The training manager could have used his telephone call with the brand manager to confront him about what role he played in helping to form the sales director's adverse view of the workshop. What factors dissuade him from adopting this course of action?

The training manager cannot be sure what role the brand manager has played in the events that preceded his receipt of the email from the sales director. He has to tread carefully for fear of making a poor situation even worse. The training manager is on the alert from the moment he hears the relaxed tone of the brand manager's voice on the phone when he calls him. The brand manager sounds unperturbed, which tells the training manager that he is quite comfortable with whatever role he has played in the events leading up to the sales director's sending her email. The training manager does not know specifically what role he did play, so he asks the brand manager two questions to see how the land lies. He asks the brand manager whether he has had a chance to give the sales director a report about the workshop. The brand manager replies that he has given her a full report, but he doesn't say anything about the nature or tone of his comments. He doesn't say if his report was broadly positive or broadly negative, just that it was full. So the training manager asks him what kind of report he has provided, and is told by the brand manager that he thinks the workshop had some positive aspects to it. This wording is deliberately evasive, and too much so for the training manager's liking. He decides that the brand manager has had a lot to do with the sales director's email, so he pushes some more. He reminds the brand manager that his parting words at the end of the workshop were friendly and positive, and that he said that the event had been useful. The brand manager is discomfited at being put on the spot. He doesn't want to be reminded of what he said at the end of the workshop, and replies with more elusive words about 'Everything in business has value' before ending the call promptly. The training manager can now be in no doubt that the brand manager has been maneuvering behind the scenes, even though he still does not know what exactly he said. This is an important conclusion for him to come to, because it helps him decide how to respond to the sales director's email. His reply is carefully worded. He gives her the full facts, telling her what was covered in the workshop. He characterizes the debate fairly as fractious at times, but points out the achievements of the event. He informs her politely but clearly that without the workshop the team and its manager would not have started to speak more openly to one another about the taboo subject of how the team is being run. He does not know to what extent the sales director will believe him, but he does know that, up until the very recent past, she has thought well of him. He hopes that his reputation will count for something in her eyes, and that she will hear the truth of his assertions. He is also quite clever in that he points out that there were a team full of people in the room, any of whom could give an account of the proceedings should she want to ask them. This is a wise point to make because it demonstrates that he has confidence in his case, and is certain anyone else in the room would make comments that corroborate his version of events, but doesn't go so far as to suggest that the version of events she has heard is either pejorative or false.

Set Five

■ What does the brand manager hope to gain by handling things in this way?

The brand manager hopes to gain two things from handling things like this. First, he wants to buy himself some time as he considers how to respond to the suggestion which was sprung on him at the workshop that he reorganize his team so that they report to two of his senior team members instead of him. He really does not like this suggestion at all. At one stroke it reduces his power and status in the team, and removes him from its day-to-day functioning. He is an able brand manager so he would enjoy the additional time spent working with retail outlets and clients that his new role would involve. But, he is a status-conscious character, and much of the way he meets this need is through his day-to-day dealings with his team members. He also has a jealous nature, and doesn't like the idea that his two most senior team members should manage the team. He thinks they might actually be better at doing this than he is, and can't afford, as he sees it, to let this situation develop.

Second, he notes the welcome that the sales director affords to the training manager. He notes her positive reaction to him, her wish for training and development to play a leading role in helping the company move forward, and her invitation to the training manager to attend the next top team meeting. He hears her invite him to speak at it, and his jealousy is piqued again. He is a brittle character, doesn't mix easily, and hasn't built much liking or respect with his peers in the top team. His relationship with the sales director, who is his boss, is predicated on his being able at managing her perceptions of him and his team, and his capacity to deliver effective brand management initiatives. He fears that the arrival of the training manager might upset his apple cart. He fears quite irrationally that the sales director might attach increasing importance to the work of the training manager and downplay the importance of his own work. He fears that his own shortcomings as a manager might be exposed if his team are asked to become more productive. His inimical nature, at once fragile and devious, devises a plan. He decides to present himself to the training manager as an ally, someone who rates him and wants him to work closely with his team. He does so as soon as the training manager is in post, to capitalize on his lack of knowledge of his new colleagues and more effectively blindside him. However, behind the scenes and following the workshop which the training manager runs for him, he manipulates the perceptions of the sales director, telling her that it was a less effective project than it had been. The sales director cannot afford to be seen to let this feedback go without acting upon it. She is sufficiently convinced by the forthright indignation with which the brand manager informs her of the workshop's content and process that she takes his comments at face value, and writes an ill-judged email to the training manager. Her mistake is that she puts her relationship with the brand manager, who she needs if she is to reach her new turnover target of a 50 percent increase, before any other consideration, and assumes that he is speaking the truth. She does not know how adversarial the brand manager is being towards the training manager, and having sent the email, cannot retract it or back down from its contents. The brand manager has achieved his two goals of damaging the reputation of the training manager and creating fog around the suggestion that he should no longer manage his team on a day-to-day basis.

■ What risks does the brand manager take in handling things as he does?

The brand manager does not care what view the training manager has of him so, as far as that relationship is concerned, he isn't taking a risk. He thinks his seniority over the training manager and his longevity in his role will be enough to safeguard him. However, he doesn't calculate that the training manager might actually be very good at his job as a team facilitator and might realize early on that the brand manager is a poor manager. Neither does he think things through sufficiently carefully with regard to his maneuverings with the sales director. He believes that he can dupe her and pull the wool over her eyes enough that she will not know for sure what did and what did not take place at the event. If it comes down to hearsay, he believes that he has her ear sufficiently in comparison with the training manager that he could sway her perception toward the view her wants her to have: that the workshop has done more harm than good and has proved to be an expensive waste of time. What he doesn't count on is the robust, factual way in which the training manager conducts himself in his email response to the sales director, and his suggestion that the sales director consults with other members of his team before finally deciding what did and what did not take place at the workshop.

Set Six

■ What is your reading of the situation in which the training manager now finds himself?

The training manager is now in limbo. He feels deceived by his internal client and unfairly judged by a senior manager. However, he does not know what to do to resolve any of these issues, and decides that the best thing to do is to wait and see. This is a wise decision even though it is an uncomfortable one to make, as it effectively renders him inactive while events take their course. For her part, the sales director wishes to let the issues which she raised in her email to the training manager remain where they are. She wants neither to address and resolve them, nor to draw a line under them. As far as she is concerned the issues are there for her to return to or not, as and when she sees fit. She takes this line for two reasons. The first is that, on reading the factual reply she receives from the training manager to her email to him, she is persuaded that some of his points are well made and sound truthful. She thinks she might have been hasty in her judgment of him and, for the first time, considers that there might be more to the brand manager than meets the eye. She thinks that he might have exaggerated the downside of the workshop and told her a version of events that he wants her to accept, rather than one which is accurate. Second, she does not want to back down or retract her comments to the training manager, which she thinks would be inappropriate given her seniority in the firm. She decides to regard the incident as closed for the time being and simply move on. She does not consider that this might be an uncomfortable way to do things as far as the training manager is concerned. She doesn't let concern for his feelings factor into her decision. She thinks it would be expedient for her to handle things by letting them ride, and she signals the fact that she has moved on by inviting the training manager to attend the next top team meeting.

■ Although he didn't know it at the time, the training manager's handling of his email exchange with the sales director helped his cause. What aspects of his writing style helped him sway her opinion about the merits of the workshop?

The training manager handles himself well in his email to the sales director. The benefits of his approach lie both in what he does say and in what he leaves unsaid. He is factual and accurate in his account of the workshop. He includes a reference to the degree of difficulty the team members had in being open with one another and their manager. However, he doesn't offer a view as to why dialogue was awkward between them. Instead, he lets the sales director form her own view that the brand manager might not be as able a manager as he would like her to think he is. Then, the training manager says that he accepts that the brand team has more work to do following the event, but also states that progress was made at the workshop. Finally, the training manager suggests that the sales director could solicit a view from any of the other people present at the workshop, but doesn't go further and say that the account she has heard from the brand manager represents false testimony. This combination of a measured response pointing out the unfairness of the wholly negative characterization of the workshop which the sales director has accepted, giving her the option of making up her own mind about what is going on, and suggesting that she could get corroboration of the facts from anyone else present, enables the sales director to save face. It also means that she learns that the training manager is more politically savvy than she might have thought him to be, given the report of the workshop provided to her by the brand manager. Overall, the sales director is pleased with the way the training manager handles her unfair complaint about him. He doesn't reply angrily, go to her office and cause a scene, call her and shout at her down the phone, or strike back at the brand manager. In fact he doesn't mention the brand manager at all in his email, which creates the impression that he isn't personalizing the issues, and is only interested in finding a fair and constructive way forward. In fact, the sales director might now consider that it is the brand manager who is guilty of personalizing issues. So the Sales director decides to leave the circumstances surrounding what did or did not happen at the workshop where they are and moves forward with her plans to utilize her new training manager and his team more widely in the company. She invites him to the next top team meeting and lets him come to his own conclusions about her attitude to him.

■ How does the training manager's handling of his relationship with the brand manager work in his favor?

The training manager surprises the brand manager in how he handles the fallout from his adversarial, abusive complaint. The brand manager expects that the training manager will, at the very least, react emotionally and further injure his reputation. but he doesn't. When he calls the brand manager, having received the email from the sales director, he adopts an understated approach. He delivers his reasonable questions in a low-key way. This is enough to take the wind out of the brand manager's sails and gives him pause for thought. He realizes that the training manager might be new in post and might not have well-developed relationships at a senior level. But he also becomes aware that the training manager might be a more astute political operator than he had imagined. The brand manager realizes that he might not have got to the training manager as easily as he thought he might, and decides to take half a step backwards. So he sends an email to the sales director in which he says that he will open up a further conversation within his team about the proposed new structure, and ask one of his team members to facilitate the discussion. This makes it look as if he is indeed trying to take good out of a bad situation, and is working constructively with the outputs of the workshop. He wants the sales director to see him in a positive light, to see him as a committed and responsible member of the workforce, and not as someone who bears a grudge against the training manager and the outcomes from the workshop he ran. Overall, the brand manager is minded to play down his feud with the training manager, so when he meets him at the top team meeting, his says hello to him and gets on with the meeting.

■ What could the training manager have done differently and better from the time he gained his promotion onwards which might have rendered him less vulnerable to the tactics of an adversarial ally?

From the moment the training manager is promoted, his working relationships change. He is no longer involved in a straightforward reporting relationship to his boss in the training team. He becomes the boss of that team, and gets involved in a series of relationships with senior internal clients who regard him as a professional adviser on training matters. He needs them and they need him, even though there are differences in their stature in the company and their organizational authority. He needs them to employ him and work constructively with him. He needs them to involve him in the life of the company. In return they need him – or someone like him – to develop their staff and help them reach their increased turnover targets. The problem for the training manager is that he wants to prove himself while simultaneously learning about a group of politically minded people with whom he is unfamiliar. In order to protect himself from the possibility that some of these people might prove to be adversarial colleagues, the training manager needs to tread cautiously. But, in order to take advantage of any opportunities to prove himself competent and capable in his new role, he will have to take some risks. The first opportunity he is offered involves working with the brand manager, who just happens to be an adversarial manager, someone with an inimical nature, which is well hidden from the training manager, who doesn't know him very well. The training manager wants to take up the opportunity. How can he do so safely?

First, he needs to listen very hard to everything the brand manager says to him from the first moment they speak. When the brand manager makes a comment that he doesn't understand, he needs to find something to say back to him. He cannot afford to let such comments pass without finding out what the brand manager means by uttering them. If necessary he needs to ask directly. For instance, the training manager must respond at the time he hears it to a comment such as the one about 'a meeting of minds.' If he doesn't put up some kind of boundary at this juncture, even one that simply says 'I don't follow you', the brand manager might be tempted to continue to push the boundary in future to see how far he can get. Second, the training manager needs to keep a written record of the objectives and processes he intends to use at the team assessment workshop, and at every other event he is asked to facilitate, so that there is clarity about what he is there to do and what is not within his remit. But he doesn't do this. Instead he works verbally with the brand manager, assuming a level of goodwill that doesn't exist. This leaves him vulnerable to the manipulations of the brand manager when he decides to give an unfairly poor report of the workshop to his boss the sales director.

Third, the training manager needs to be much more proactive in building relationships at the top of the company. He doesn't create opportunities to discuss his work and approach with any of his new senior managers, but contents himself with a series of one-hour introductions that they have initiated with him. When he is asked by the sales director to meet with her a second time or to attend top team meetings, he does do so. But he doesn't initiate contact with his key clients, and so misses the opportunity to build his profile with them on his terms. He is, of course, conscious that they are a busy group of people and that they have more authority than him. But, by making a point of requesting their time to talk through issues he wants to raise – issues such as the way he will work with them to raise the company's turnover, asking them what they look for in an internal supplier, agreeing with them what frequency of contact they will have with one another, and over what issues they will touch base – he would present himself as someone who is comfortable operating independently of the senior team and in tandem with them, rather than as someone who simply responds to their agenda and does what they ask him to do. Last, the training manager needs to recognize the fragile nature of the adversarial alliances at the top of the organization. Each member of the top team is in an adversarial alliance with each other member of the top team. There is very little trust amongst this group of people, and they extend little or no support to one another. They are closed with one another, even secretive, and the training manager needs to recognize that, no matter how the brand manager or the sales director present themselves when they are with him, their relationships with one another constitute a series of fragile alliances, which at this early stage of his new role, he will not understand and cannot afford to misjudge. He needs to handle each top team member with caution, not take anything for granted and not assume anything until it is proven.

References and Recommended Reading

REFERENCES

Chapter 2: The Impact of Adversarial Behaviour at Work

A. Oade (2009) *Managing Politics at Work: The Essential Toolkit for Identifying and Handling Political Behaviour in the Workplace*, Palgrave Macmillan, ISBN 978-0-230-595415

A. Oade (2009) *Managing Workplace Bullying: How To Identify, Respond To and Manage Bullying Behaviour in the Workplace*, Palgrave Macmillan, ISBN 978-0-230-228085

Chapter 3: Low Trust, Low Support

A. Oade (2009) *Managing Politics at Work: The Essential Toolkit for Identifying and Handling Political Behaviour in the Workplace*, Chapter 10, pp 130–47, Palgrave Macmillan, ISBN 978-0-230-595415

Chapter 4: Working with Adversarial Peers

A. Oade (2009) *Managing Politics at Work: The Essential Toolkit for Identifying and Handling Political Behaviour in the Workplace*, Chapter 8, pp 99–107, Palgrave Macmillan, ISBN 978-0-230-595415

RECOMMENDED READING

P. Babiak and R. D. Hare (2007) *Snakes in Suits: When Psychopaths Go To Work*, Harper Collins, ISBN 978-0-061-147890

M. Buckingham (2005) *First Break All The Rules*, Pocket Books, ISBN 978-1-416-502661

C. Coffman and G. Gonzalez-Molina (2003) *Follow This Path: How The World's Greatest Organisations Unleash Human Potential*, Random House Business Books, ISBN 978-1-844-130122

Peter J. Frost (2007) *Toxic Emotions at Work and What You Can Do About Them*, Harvard Business School Press, ISBN 978-1-4221-0285-5

L. R. Libove and E. M. Russo (1997) *Trust: The Ultimate Test*, HRDQ, Organisation Design and Development Inc

A. Oade (2009) *Managing Politics at Work: The Essential Toolkit for Identifying and Handling Political Behaviour in the Workplace*, Palgrave Macmillan, ISBN 978-0-230-595415

A. Oade (2009) *Managing Workplace Bullying: How To Identify, Respond To and Manage Bullying Behaviour in the Workplace*, Palgrave Macmillan, ISBN 978-0-230-228085

A. Oade (2010) *Building Influence in the Workplace: How To Gain and Retain Influence at Work*, Palgrave Macmillan, ISBN 978-0-230-237735

K. Reivich and A. Shatté (2002) *The Resilience Factor: Essential Skills for Overcoming Life's Inevitable Obstacles*, Broadway Books, ISBN 978-0-767-911900

M. Stout (2005) *The Sociopath Next Door*, Broadway Books, ISBN 978-0-767-915823

Index

A

Adversarial alliances, 21, 55, 160, 161–91

Adversarial behaviour, case studies, 8–11, 11–16, 22–6, 28–32, 43–6, 51–6, 56–60, 61–3, 69–75, 84–9, 91–7, 100–3, 105–9, 112–16, 118–21, 133–6, 139–43, 145–51, 155–7, 161–91

Adversarial behaviour, challenges of, 26–7, 40–1

Adversarial behaviour, consequences of, 2, 6–8, 17–22, 27–8, 68–9

Adversarial behaviour, definition of, 3–4, 18

Adversarial behaviour, examples of, 7, 20, 21–2, 27–8, 68, 99–100, 103–5, 129–33, 137–9, 143–5

Adversarial behaviour, selective, 49–66

Adversarial behaviour, your experience, 1–4

Adversarial bullies, 17–19

Adversarial colleagues, 3–5, 20–2

Adversarial colleagues, your, 32–4, 47–8, 64–5, 83–4, 97, 1110–11, 123, 136–7, 154–5

Adversarial managers, aim of, 137–138

Adversarial managers, challenge of working for, 138–9, 157–9

Adversarial managers, impact of, 131–3, 139–43

Adversarial managers, reporting to, 123–36, 155–9

Adversarial managers, use of authority, 129–30

Adversarial mindsets, 4–8, 143–5

Adversarial team members, 99–124

Adversarial team members, confronting, 105–10

Adversarial team members, giving feedback to, 56–60, 121–3

Adversarial team members, managing, 56–60, 99–124

Adversarial peers, working alongside, vii, 22–26, 28–32, 51–6, 67–98, 125

Adversarial politicians, 17–19

Authoritarian behaviour, 54, 166, 182

Authority, antagonism towards, 116–17, 124

B

Boundaries, viii, xi, 10, 20, 21, 28, 37, 46, 50, 58, 60, 61–4, 65, 68, 69–72, 76–82, 83, 98, 138–9, 152–4, 157, 159, 190, 191

Boundary conflicts, 61–4, 68–72, 76–82

Bullying behaviour, 17–19

Burnout zone, 38–9, 46

C

Challenge at work, 37–9

Comfort zone, 38–9

Commitment, demonstrating, 21, 40, 59, 81, 82, 96, 140, 148, 149

Commitment, lack of, 4, 20, 41, 79, 84, 138

Competitive behaviour, xii, 20, 49, 50, 52, 152, 154

Compliance, mitigating the risks of, 152–4

Control issues, 4, 18, 19, 44, 68, 76, 77, 82–3, 95, 98, 102, 103, 108–11, 120, 150, 179

D

Disagreement, 7, 52, 86, 91, 100–3, 126, 145, 162, 166

E

Effective performance, 38, 40

Enemies, workplace, 5, 6, 27, 50, 51–6, 145–51

Escalating issues, 8, 53, 84, 89, 131

Ethical boundaries, 128

F

Feedback issues, 20, 21, 57, 60, 69, 80, 99, 104, 108, 112, 121–3, 124, 129, 130, 131, 140, 166, 180

I

Integrity, 21, 36, 143, 156

Integrity, lack of, 9, 91

Integrity, maintaining, 131, 151, 157

Irresponsible behaviour, 15, 19, 75

M

Managers, adversarial, 125–60

Managers, non-adversarial, 127–9

Manipulative behaviour, 55, 100, 180, 186, 191

N

Naming the game, 109–10

Non-adversarial behaviour, vii, 4, 6, 16, 24, 26, 34, 37, 48, 49, 50, 51, 55–8, 61–4, 65, 76–81, 89, 124, 125, 127–30, 159

Non-performance, 38, 39, 112–16

O

Oppositional behaviour, vii, 1, 3, 5, 7, 9, 17–34, 40, 41, 48, 49, 64, 71, 76, 78, 80, 82, 83–90, 91–7, 99–124, 148, 151, 158, 179

Organizational authority, 21, 30, 50, 51, 54, 66, 67–98, 99–124, 125–60, 162, 181, 190, 191

P

Peers, adversarial, vii, 22–6, 28–32, 51–6, 67–98, 125

Perceptions, managing, 42, 54, 55, 60, 104, 114, 140, 145, 156, 179, 186–7

Political behaviour, 5, 17–19, 31, 36, 42, 58, 60, 81, 160, 161–4, 167, 172, 180, 183, 188, 190, 193

Power dynamics, viii, 18, 19, 26, 53–6, 64, 65, 72, 75, 125–31, 139, 140, 159, 178, 179, 185

R

Rapport, 6, 42, 103, 142

Reputation, adversarial, 69, 71–3

Reputation, building a, xiii, 69, 112, 120

Reputational risk, 7, 18, 54, 68, 75, 77–8, 82, 94, 100, 109, 122, 174, 180, 189

Responsibility towards colleagues, 4, 9, 10, 14, 20, 21, 41, 58, 63, 76, 99

Risk, placing oneself at, 5, 19, 131, 135

Risk, managing, 67–98, 143, 152–4

S

Selective adversarial behaviour, 49–66

Supportive behaviour at work, 35–48, 116

Support, different expressions of, 42–3

Support, low levels of, 1–16, 17–19, 26, 27, 35–48, 129, 132–3, 138–9, 143, 144

T

Team members, adversarial, 56–60, 99–124

Transactional behaviour, 3, 5, 9, 10, 11, 14

Trust at work, 35–48

Trust, low levels of, 1–16, 17–19, 26, 27, 35–48, 129, 132–3, 138–9, 143, 144

Trust, working without, 40–1, 43–6

Trustworthiness, 36, 37, 44, 46, 47–8, 53, 76, 79, 116

U

Unsupportive behaviour, xi, 9, 14, 20, 21, 98, 179

Untrustworthiness, 5, 9, 10, 14, 68, 81, 98

V

Values, personal, 19, 93, 96, 128, 129

Values, examples of adversarial, 143–5

Vulnerability, professional, 37, 45, 177